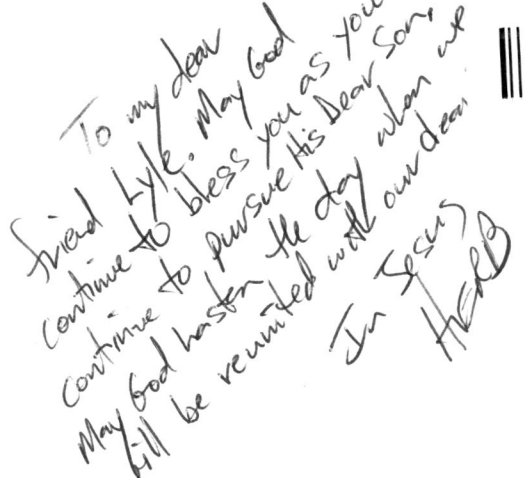
AF207407

FALLING IN
LOVE WITH
JESUS

HERB LARSEN JR

FALLING IN LOVE WITH JESUS

TASH Publishing and Distribution
35276 Rockwell Dr
Abbotsford, British Columbia V3G 2C9
Canada

Edited by Marilyn Morgan and Clifford Goldstein.

Published by TASH Publishing and Distribution, 35276 Rockwell Dr, Abbotsford, British Columbia, Canada V3G 2C9

Printed in Singapore by KHL Printing Co Pte Ltd

Cover design by Alicia Jurek/iStockPhoto.com
Text design by Lee Dunstan/Shane Winfield
Typeset in 12.5/17 Adobe Caslon Pro.

Larsen, Herb, 1955–
Falling in Love With Jesus
ISBN: 978-0-9923499-0-5

CONTENTS

DEDICATION

*This book is dedicated to the memory of my dear
mother, Lorraine Larsen, who so selflessly gave of her life's energy
to ensure that her three sons had every creative advantage in life.
In addition, she had read and reread the early drafts of this book,
all the time applying her giftedness in the mechanics of the English
language. May our separation in this life be one of brevity as we
wait for the soon return of our Lord and Saviour Jesus Christ.*

*And to my dear father, Herb Larsen Sr., without whose
example as a dynamic preacher, a loving patriarch, and a
supportive mentor, I would have almost certainly never
found myself on the path of world-wide public ministry.
You continue to serve as an earthly rock upon whom I rely
when times are rough, as well as when they're good.*

*I thank God daily that I was blessed with such giving
parents, recognizing that to be raised in a home where
the dominating atmosphere is that of unity and
Godly love is a rarity to be treasured always.*

FOREWORD

SERENDIPITY PLAYS OUT IN THE LIFE OF ANYONE WHO IS dedicated to the cause of Christ. (My friend, Herb, calls this "a God thing.") So I don't recall the point at which I became involved in the production of this book. But I suspect it was some years before a more recent fortuitous encounter in a church carpark with Russell Fehlberg, point man for Herb Larsen Ministries in Australia, when, experiencing a sudden rush of blood to the head, I volunteered my editorial services and printing contacts for the publication of this book.

I'd gotten to know Herb as he shared fishing stories across a dining table during various of his many speaking engagements across Australia, but more so from his elegantly simple and powerful message of how to get to know—how to develop a life-changing relationship—with Christ, the subject of this book.

I can endorse his message, for I know that Herb's practical, plain-speak, inspiring message has changed lives, my own included, and impacted others.

At one particular campmeeting, in the by then overcrowded tent (the alternate adult tent was embarrassingly empty), and a few nights into his series, I sat listening to Herb. With me, having attended each night, was a friend who rarely darkened a church doorway but came with me the first night and returned for more. Disillusioned because of some shabby treatment from her local church, she'd thrown it all in, and only went to church when I was in town.

"So, would you go to church if Herb was your minister?" I enquired at the conclusion of the meeting.

"Of course, Lee," she said. "Why do you think I'm here?"

She, like Herb, loves to fish, and so was keen to meet him. The two developed a conversation, swapping fish tails.

Herb's transparent, biblical and amazingly simple message, along with an authentic Christianity, penetrates where nothing else does. This message is outlined in the pages that follow. It's about how to build and maintain a relationship with Christ that will so transform your life that in a year you may not recognize yourself. It is elegant in its simplicity and easy to understand, even if not so easy to implement. Rather, it takes time and dedication, perspiration and sacrifice, seeking God with *all* one's heart.

But for the true seeker, the one who tries and trusts, a result is guaranteed. And it's yours if you care to try.

—*Lee Dunstan*
Sydney, Australia

CHAPTER 1

ALTAR CALL

IT IS ONE OF THE FEW EVENTS IN MY LIFE THAT STILL FEELS as if it took place only yesterday. I was attending a Christian high school, and our school was wrapping up another spiritual emphasis week. During this week, a guest speaker preached to us for thirty minutes each morning on spiritual topics that were meant to draw students into making life-long commitments to following God. Although I can no longer recall the specific content of his series, I do remember, rather vividly, his call for commitment at the end of his lectures.

He had obviously done a good enough job of preparing my mind for his passionate altar call (when a preacher asks people to show their commitment to God by walking down to the front of the church in a public profession of faith) because my emotions were churning and burning me up. Part of me cried out to finally give up on self and give my all to Jesus, while the other part was being driven by human logic, which was boldly exposing every reason why this would be detrimental, if not fatal, to my lifelong goals and aspirations.

The students had been taken to hell and back several times that week through the speaker's sermons, as they were very often used as fear-factor ploys in order to get us to make a quick and decisive decision for Jesus. And, for sure, fear was there, as God was once again exposed as an exacting slave driver waiting to beat me over the head with the possibility of not making the right decision and, therefore, foregoing the glorious reward of the Christian: eternal life.

As a church-going, long-haired and fashion-conscious young person, I had been at this crossroad many times before. With a background of Christian school attendance since grade one, and the minimum of one spiritual emphasis week-of-prayer per school year (not counting all the spiritual revivals away from school)—I had become both accustomed to, as well as had developed disdain for, the dreaded altar call.

Many things were going on at once: there existed that undeniable perpetual trauma caused by the internal battle between right and wrong that exists in all of us; the heavy-handed psychological head-games used by some preachers to motivate a decision; the horrific negative force caused by peer-pressure to conform to my friends' world rather than to God's; and the trenchant observation that most of the people I knew in positions of spiritual influence in the church were (in my opinion), duds.

Then, against the backdrop of someone laboriously playing, like a scratched record, thirty repetitions of "I Surrender All" on the chapel's electronic organ, the preacher began to beg and plead for one more "lost" soul to walk down the aisle. My mind, as usual, became a jumbled mess: *What would all my friends think if I stood up like a stooge and walked the long aisle to the front? What would this do to my high goals and aspirations? What about my reputation as a tough guy, the sports jock type?* Plus, I had every intention of being someone great in life—someone who was going to make an impact on the world with money, success and notoriety as the indicator. *Was I ready to cash it all in over a decision that would certainly limit those goals?*

Questions, dozens of them, without any answers flooded my scrambled mind. To say that there was, at a minimum, a ferocious battle for possession of my mind would have been an understatement. How I wanted to experience the abundant life the Bible talked so unsparingly about. And yet, through observation, I concluded that such promises worked only in Bible times. Looking around at my fellow church-going members, and carefully observing the lives of those who were church leaders, I had previously wanted nothing to do with any of it.

In an attempt to clear my mind of the blood-splattered, chaotic war brewing in my head, I decided to focus all my attention on exactly what the preacher was offering me by way of his passionate pitch. Yes, there it was again. I had heard it many times before. He was talking of the abundant life promised, the good life, the life filled with rich experience and joy. It was where the action was supposed to be, and not what the world offered, which was only temporary anyway. This I truly wanted but, for some reason, couldn't buy as truth because I had a difficult time at that point trying to recall anyone, outside that of my own loving parents, that I would consider as fitting the bill of living some kind of "great life." Most of the people I knew as supposedly "good Christians" were long-faced, critical, and judgmental and they lived what seemed to be boring and empty lives, or so it seemed.

The Long Walk

Driven by the hope above all hopes that I would get something in return for a positive decision, I pushed logic into the deep recesses of my mind and slowly let myself gravitate towards giving in to Jesus, with the glimmer of expectation that just, maybe, I could or would experience a joy I had never seen nor felt before.

OK, I like what the preacher is offering, so what is it I now have to do to get it?

As if it were an answer to my question alone, these words came out of his mouth, words that I have heard so many times before: "Just simply give your heart to the Lord."

Yeah, yeah. I know that. But how do I actually go about giving away my heart—because that idea, at a minimum, is a bizarre if not a completely abstract thought?

Again the answer came from the preacher, as if for me only: "Just get up out of your seat, walk down the aisle to the front where I and some of your teachers will meet you to get your names and then make plans to have you go through a series of Bible studies so that you can become a candidate for baptism."

My mind once again began to swim with a torrent of questions: *Why is it that this solution seems too simple to be true? What about all those endless rules and regulations that I was brought up trying to keep? Do I simply ignore the rigor with which I have been taught to adhere to them?*

As the call wore on, I was eventually left with only one argument: *How do I know it won't work when I have never given it a try?*

With knees near buckling from the adrenaline rush produced by the trauma of the internal battle, I finally and decisively stood up and asked to be excused as I clamored over people's legs. Once free, I focused my attention on the front of the chapel and made my way down that seemingly mile-long aisle, where a bunch of other kids already stood, those whom I had generally viewed as the school nerds. Immediately my heart began to pound from both the sense of relief, as well as the feeling of excitement at the peace that quickly overwhelmed me. Something truly was happening. I was now standing up front in a bold public statement of my faith in Jesus, and it definitely felt good and empowering.

As expected, our school chaplain asked that I write down my name and phone number; he would be getting in touch with me to discuss Bible study. I complied and then walked away, feeling emotionally as light as a feather. Even the air I breathed felt fresher and more invigorating. The huge weight of my years of indecisiveness was now lifted from my tormented shoulders; I felt as if I could walk on water. For probably the first time in my life, I could honestly care less what my friends thought of my public display of faith in Jesus.

I was about to embark on a new and exciting journey.

CHAPTER 2

RUNNING ON EMPTY

I WENT HOME THAT AFTERNOON WITH JOY IN MY HEART, BUT a strange thing happened: I couldn't bring myself to share this news with my parents. I was, after all, a preacher's kid. My loving parents would have been over-joyed but there was some sort of a mental block that simply said, *I can't do it.* Most of that night, as I lay awake in my bed, my head was swimming with scenarios, and with questions that had, it seemed, few answers. The biggest was, *Now what? What is my life going to be like from now on? What have I given up or sacrificed?* After all, I had thoroughly envisioned myself as being hugely successful in life. And then there was the unanswered and nagging question, *Why couldn't I share the news with my dear parents?*

My dad was a very successful church pastor and administrative leader, a dynamic speaker and motivator. My mom was hugely creative in music and art and had a host of other strong character attributes.

She was also completely self-sacrificing about making sure that her children had every advantage possible in all the arts (visual art, music, etcetera), as well as in other life-enriching pursuits.

Ultimately, that phobia against sharing what was supposed to be good news had everything to do with my conditioned belief that in God's eye I could never claim any victory until I'd actually proved something to Him. I believed, through years of observation—not preaching and teaching—that I needed to be at least walking the straight and narrow before Jesus could or would accept me. Through the emphasis I'd been subject to—that of adhering to the commands of the Bible as well as church—I, through religious osmosis believed, contrary to both the teachings of my parents as well as the Bible, that I had first to become good before I could come to Jesus. And certainly everyone, especially my parents, knew that I'd done a good job of upholding the universal stereotype of PKs (preacher's kid). I was, after all, given the generous expectation, by fellow parishioners, that I would automatically become a typical PK; that is, I would morph into a teenage hellion for at least a third of my life before, hopefully, moving back to center. (Isn't it funny how young people sometimes rise or fall to the level of expectation people around them pin on their names?). To then report to my parents that I had made a commitment to follow Jesus when they, above anyone else, knew that I wasn't fit or ready for such a serious step was, in my mind, to sound almost blasphemous to God. I felt that before I could share the good news of my decision, I needed to fulfill one big prerequisite, that I would first need to abandon all worldly thought and pursuit and then show some great strides towards spirituality—all before I could legitimately divulge my long delayed decision.

Regrets

I went to bed that first night with my mind racing with thoughts—thoughts of the future, thoughts of the past and most certainly thoughts related to reliving my walk to the front of the chapel that very day. Sleep eluded me for most of the night, as I could not, for the life of me, shut my mind off from considering what my new life might look like now that I had supposedly given my heart to Jesus.

Hours into that first restless night, I did finally fall asleep but, when I awoke—it was to a feeling of desperation. Like a rifle blast, a shot of adrenaline exploded through my veins. The elation I had felt the day before was now, instantaneously, replaced by a gigantic dose of regret. The ramification of my decision to give my heart to Jesus hit me square in the face. I felt my dreams of making it big in the fields of art, music, writing, and sports were gone. I had truly planned on being someone important, but now it was as though I were about to enter the most dreaded realm of conformism known to man—that of becoming a church-going zealot.

Already, I simply wished I could back out. But how?

I got out of bed, took a shower, dressed, and joined my parents and two brothers for breakfast. Looking at my parents, I quickly became thankful that I hadn't shared my news with them, as that would have buried me even deeper. Once at school, I saw many of my friends and felt so glad they didn't say anything about what happened yesterday. But then I saw the chaplain and thought, *Oh, no! Please don't make a big deal about it especially in front of my friends.*

Obviously, my wishes were not to be fulfilled. He bee-lined straight to me and with a big public handshake congratulated me on my decision and, then, promptly set about trying to create a schedule for Bible studies. I gave every excuse I could think of as to why I couldn't fit this time slot or that. Fortunately, I was able to leave that stressful encounter without having committed to anything. I just simply hoped he would lose interest and go away but, like a fruit fly to rotten fruit, he began pursuing me over the next couple of weeks. Though I remember little of what happened afterward, I did eventually wind up studying with him, but it had to have been pretty much a formality, as I remember nothing of what I might have learned there. Nevertheless, whatever took place through those meaningless get-togethers, I was now prepared for the pinnacle of all "rights of passage," that of baptism.

Baptism

It was early springtime when we, my two brothers, a cousin and I, as well as many of our family and friends, made our way to a small lake near Mount Rainier in the state of Washington, where we then lived. Of course, with the cool of high elevation, coupled with the fact that the lake had sat under a sheet of ice for the last couple of months, the water was going to be freezing. It was. I tried desperately to focus on the beautifully symbolic experience rather than the physical shock of being submersed in the frigid water, and to my amazement, I again felt an incredible feeling of peace engulf my body as I waded to shore and then to a warm cabin to change into dry clothes.

My heart so wanted to be free of the huge pressure I had placed on myself over my worldly goals and aspirations and yet, undeniably, the preparation my parents gave my brothers and me to succeed in life told me that I could become anything and accomplish anything I ever chose. Thus, I perpetually allowed myself the freedom to think: *Wouldn't it be wonderful if God were to bless me with success as well as a relationship with Him?*

In spite of the fact that I strongly believed that the life of the Christian was to be one of unending sacrifice, I also held firmly to the hope that the offer of eternal life in a place called Heaven would be worth the perceived quasi-hell I must live through here on earth while engaging in a religious life. Certainly, my belief was based around one whereby, as a supposedly dedicated Christian, I would be forced into a boring life of conformism and sacrifice in order to get my earned reward later. Now that I was a baptized Christian, at least that's what I thought I was, I began a life of waiting for the supposed benefits of Christianity to kick in and overwhelm me the abundant life always talked of but rarely seen. Discouragingly, the "abundant life" never seemed to show its face in any way, shape or form in my new life.

Going Through the Motions

As I set out on my new venture of being a supposedly committed Christian, I made sure that I did all the things the best self-proclaimed Christians did. I rigidly attended church every week, even during those times when I had a great excuse not to go (such as illness, relatives in town, or maybe a snowy blizzard). But one thing was for sure, at the end of every week, you could count on the fact that there would be a check mark in the heavenly record of church attendance for Herb Larsen. In fact, church attendance sort of became my "Dow Jones" of monitoring my spiritual-investment-performance.

I also began paying tithe to my church on every bit of money I earned, even the little bit of cash I would get from mowing a lawn. After all, great would be my reward in Heaven; but, even more importantly, I would get a whole heap of money as a return on investment now, at least that is what I understood.

In addition, I made a gallant effort to not use foul language or to "drop the gloves" (fighting) when someone would cheap-shot me while playing hockey, or any number of other competitive sports I engaged in. Of course, body-slamming them in righteous retaliation was part of the acceptable rules of the game; thus, I could certainly practice behavior within the guidelines of whatever sport I was playing. And there was always the fact that if my actions were considered a bit excessive by the referees, I would graciously (sometimes) serve my time in the penalty box and, thereby, erase all condemnation.

I also, rather rigidly, abstained from getting too close to, or hanging out with, the "wrong" crowd. I was, after all, instructed, through the sermons I would listen to at church, that purity was a virtue and, because the world is filthy—don't go near it (at least that seemed to be the message I got).

To be honest, though, for many years I was simply going through the motions, with only one return-on-investment on the blurry distant horizon: my hope that, whatever I had to go through here, Heaven would be worth the wait.

Discontent

Despite my fears about what my faith would do to my life-pursuits—as I moved on into adult life, I did eventually have huge success in all my worldly pursuits. Virtually every single endeavor I engaged in, very quickly turned into huge success with validation being given by many articles being written in newspapers and magazines about my accomplishments. I became a published author. I gained international notoriety for my gun and knife engraving as well as the visual arts with drawings, paintings and lithographs being sold in most of North America's art centers as well as commissions from important people in society including Hollywood celebrities. I illustrated books and magazines for many notable publishers including Canada's largest, Gage Publishing. Music, that of composing and arranging as well as performing, also came without a hitch to me.

Yet, even with the money, the accolades, the articles written, the rubbing of shoulders with celebrities, millionaires, billionaires, high-level political types—none of it brought me one shred of the contentment and peace of mind that I was seeking. Nothing I had acquired or accomplished was enough, and I quickly came to the ugly realization that no matter what I achieved, it would not satisfy me. When I began to realize that the true sense of contentment I so yearningly sought was not to be found, that it was something illusive or unachievable within the framework of worldly pursuit and accomplishment, I had only one other place to turn, and that was to my so-called faith.

Unfortunately, that particular pursuit also fell drastically short of all my expectations. In addition to coming up empty-handed in my worldly endeavors, as far as inner contentment was concerned, I was also failing miserably in my spiritual journey. Suffice to say, after many gallant attempts to get God's attention, such as co-directing a health-lecture/cooking school with a professional body builder; getting involved in many of the service-oriented aspects of church life as well as eventually cofounding, with my wife and four other people, a highly successful church plant—I finally reached my make-or-break level. I had every reason to believe that to start a church and see it explode in attendance would be an act that would have drawn me into God's "inner circle" of those who matter most to Him. It had everything to do with I could no longer simply play the church game, that of getting together every weekend for a couple of hours to sit back like knots on a log and listen as the preacher presented Bible theory accompanied by little to no real modern-day proof. Yes, there were miracles taking place every day that should have more than suggested that God was alive and well and that Jesus' sacrifice on Calvary was powerful enough to free those in bondage. Yes, I was there to preach, to counsel, to plan, to write dramas and music, and to attend meetings. Yes, the stories of those who, after years of "wandering in the wilderness", were returning to God through this new church, were simply mind-blowing in nature. But it seemed as if I were standing on the periphery of it all.

As a lay preacher-leader, I began wrestling with the thought that I was nothing but a fraud. I was preaching about the benefits of a relationship with Jesus and watching as it worked in other's lives but, in that department, I was perpetually running flat out on empty. Indeed, amid the huge void that I harbored, I had actually developed a jealously and resentment towards those new converts who were flocking into our church and obviously finding something real in Jesus. How could it be that a church leader, like myself, was not entitled to or privy to experiencing the rebirth that seemed to be granted so beautifully to everyone else? Something had to change. And it was obvious what: *me!*

CHAPTER 3

LET'S MAKE A DEAL

THUS, AT THIS STAGE OF MY LIFE, MY BIGGEST QUESTION was, *What will it take to finally secure that seemingly elusive connection with a seemingly distant and unfamiliar God?* Then, interestingly, a few words of advice attributed to Mother Teresa among others, started me off in a new direction. She, simply, stated, "Spend one hour a day in adoration of the Lord and you'll be all right."

Whatever theological differences I may have had with her faith tradition was beside the point. What mattered was that the simplicity found in Mother Teresa's formula for spiritual success hit me right between the eyes. It seemed so simple, even though finding an extra hour in each of my already desperately short days was not going to be that easy. Yet the wide road leading to the abundant successes found in my worldly pursuits had, hideously, wound up being a dead-end street, while the narrow pathway I was attempting to navigate that supposedly led to spirituality simply

14

fizzled into a wall of impassable jungle. It was do or die—one last try—or get out.

The Deal

Out of desperation, I was now ready to make one last deal with God, a deal that would determine whether or not my future would include Him or whether I would openly, without any more pretense, do my own thing. After having thought long and hard as to whether I was ready to take the plunge of commitment through an hour spent each day, I finally informed God of what my deal would look like. This was my ultimatum to the Creator of the Universe: I was going to spend an hour a day with Him, and He had better come to me in a very real way, or I am done with it all.

This deal was different than what I had ever presented God before. First, all my deals with God were like this: *God, if You do this for me, I will do that for You. In other words, Give me something first, so when I have it in my hand, I can give some of it back to you.*

The disconcerting part of all my deals with God in the past was that God never seemed to, even once, reciprocate. Not until one day did I finally figure out, through direct Bible study, that my deals with God were nearly always completely backwards to the cause and effect as established by Him. What I eventually discovered was that "God never promises that which you have not already given."

For example, looking at the promise of Luke 6:38, where it states an order of events, we read: "Give, and it will be given to you: good measure, pressed down, shaken together, and running over will be put into your bosom. For with the same measure that you use, it will be measured back to you." To understand the principle of cutting a deal with God, we need to pay close attention to who does what first. According to this verse, who gives first, God or me?

There should be no question as to the answer to the question asked. I am to give first and then, and only then, can I expect something in return from God. The great thing is, the return is promised to not just be a refilling of the cup I emptied on God's behalf, but rather a refilling that "runs over," in other words, I am to get back more than I gave in the first place.

As further examples of the order in which God's promises are predicated, what about James 4:8 were it states, "Draw near to God and He will draw near to you," or Luke 6:37: "Forgive, and you will be forgiven." And Matthew 7:2: "For with what judgment you judge, you will be judged; and with the measure you use, it will be measured back to you."

Radically different than what I had mistakenly understood before was that of, there can be no return on investment if I am unwilling to first invest something. A return can only come if and when something was first given. Put another way, if I am not willing to invest in God's kingdom by way of first granting favor to someone else, then how can I, in all honesty, expect favor to come roaring my way?

The Real Deal

To understand the biblical principle of "Let's make a deal," I simply needed to establish the order of who does what and when. What I had failed to see was that cutting deals with God begins with my doing something first, not the other way around. In other words, God needs to know that I am willing to uphold my end of the deal first before he can trust me with His end of the deal. It's like this: if before I am rich, I exercise compassion on others and give of what very little I may have, then I am put in a position to have to trust that God will replenish my meager coffers which leads to the whole concept of who needs to have faith in whom. If I expect God to first give to me, then inherently, He has to have faith in me that I will reciprocate. On the other hand, if I liberally give first, whether it be money, time, talent or energy, then it is I who needs to have faith in Him, that He will replenish that which I have already given away.

That critical understanding led me to cut a new kind of deal with God. Yes, it was the Holy Spirit who prompted me to make the move to develop a relationship with the Almighty, but I first needed to respond to that prompting in order for any kind of action to take place. The point is, with my new understanding of how God works, that I needed to make a move first, I ventured into my ultimatum with Him, realizing that I would have to get up earlier in the morning if I were to find the needed time. That meant I had to get up at 5:30 AM, tough for a guy who loved to stay up very late and then sleep later in the morning.

I had now related my terms of the deal: I would spend one hour every morning, praying my guts out and reading Scripture in search of answers to my spiritual frustration. In response, God would have to make my life explode with relevance and purpose. I wanted to see miracles happening around me, as did the disciples in the book of Acts. I wanted the feeling of completeness and bold power that Bible characters like David, Daniel and Solomon had experienced. In short, I wanted direction and relevance. And if God did not come through with His end of the bargain, I would walk away from a God I truly believed to be real but never experienced.

To believe, however, that God is real, and yet to feel that He is somehow untouchable was more than I could bear.

Nada, Zilch, Nothing

Now, it wasn't that I hadn't spent time reading the Bible or praying before. I had done both. But there was always an agenda: I needed material for a sermon, or for some other church-related activity, or the like. Now, though, there was one motive only: a true relationship with Jesus.

I remember well the very private anticipation I had as I responded to the annoying alarm clock that first morning. But I got up, showered, dressed, and went into my study. I expected something incredible to happen there, a "mighty rushing wind" or the like, as seen in the book of Acts. Because this was a deal revolving around time, I began by looking at my watch and then started praying. As it was, that part of the one hour probably lasted no more than about four or five minutes before I found myself quickly prayed out of subject matter. Furthermore, my mind was wandering all over, from things like what I forgot to do yesterday to the most mundane business issues.

I then opened my Bible. As I began to read, my mind was hyper-alert to the potential that God was going to reward this, my new deal, with a manifestation of Himself as I have had never had before. I read for one whole hour to the minute and then put the Bible away and, much to my great angst—got zero out of it. Nada. Zilch. Nothing. I had even tried the age-old trick of just flipping the Bible open to some random place and then letting my eyes rest on the page in hopes that God would speak to me with a perfectly selected Bible verse. But, again, nothing happened, nothing showed up as being relevant or providential.

Of course I was hugely disappointed, if not even more disillusioned than before. But I was not going to give up easily because, as I have said, this was my final shot before I walked out on God.

As difficult as it was to be rudely awakened the next morning at 5:30 AM by my alarm clock, I begrudgingly crawled out of bed, showered and again made my way upstairs. I again looked at my watch to mark the start time; again spent one hour, to the minute, praying and reading the Bible; and, again, I got not one shred of inspiration out of it. My huge disappointment was beginning to overwhelm me to where I didn't even want to think about trying another day of this nonsense, but my ancestral roots of being fifty percent stubborn Norwegian and 50 percent bull-headed German for once was going to become useful. I would keep this up, no matter what.

As I faithfully spent my hour each morning in prayer and Bible study, nothing new came to me; nor did I feel the real presence of God. In fact, the opposite happened: it seemed the more time I expended in attempting to ultimately experience Him in a concrete and real way, the more distant and spiritually irrelevant I felt.

At a point of about a month and a half into my deal with God, after not having missed a single minute of my pledged hour each morning—I was so confused and frustrated that I wanted to walk right then and there, but I decided that too much was at stake, so I was not going to give up—not quite yet anyhow. In addition, as human nature is, I became obsessed with that which I wanted yet could not have. I actually became obsessed with the constant and nagging question, *Why can't I have you, Jesus?*

Going Down Fast

One week turned into two, then three, then six weeks of never missing a morning of spending an hour in prayer and Bible reading. Nothing, not even a divine nudge, came my way though. Over the approximately next two weeks (week six to week eight), I actually did notice something happening. Not only was frustration at not being able to connect with God overwhelming me, but also there was a very real sense that God was withdrawing His presence from me, and I actually felt emptier and emptier as time and pursuit went on. So strong was this feeling of abandonment that I would lie wide awake most nights with thoughts of disillusionment churning and burning me up. Also, during the day, when work was to be my necessity, I was so consumed with the thought, "Why can't I have you, Jesus?" that I could not accomplish even the most basic of work-related functions. An all-consuming question hideously plagued me that whole two weeks, that of, how was it that I not only didn't sense a new and better life coming on but instead was left to feel as if God were becoming more distant to me than ever before?

The answer to that question and reality would later be given to me of which answer I will share through the remainder of this book. Amid my now passionate pursuit of something that cruelly eluded me, I began oscillating between two thought processes. First, I was consumed by the disturbing and confusing thought of, "If you, God, are actually real, then why can't I experience you?" And, then, when I felt no answer to that question, I would entertain the chilling conclusion that, "Maybe everything I was ever taught and believed in, regarding God, was nothing more than a lie or a cruel myth."

I recognize, today, that it was only through the prompting of the

Holy Spirit that I even chose to hang in there for any period of time beyond a couple of fruitless days. Finally, though, after two months to the day of never missing an hour in the morning, I concluded that this deal was not worth pursuing any longer. Thus, exactly sixty days after commencing my deal with God, I awoke and made my way upstairs. I didn't feel like sitting nor kneeling to pray that morning as those associated physical stances just didn't correlate with my feelings. I, instead, literally laid down on the floor, clenched my fists and began to vent my pent-up frustration with God for His lack of response to my years, as well as more recently, weeks, of yearning for Him.

I told God that I was no longer interested in Him and that I was ending my pursuit. I told Him that I wasn't even sure if He was real anymore and that, if He were, I didn't care. After venting a much more graphic prayer than related here, I lay there awhile in utter despondency, wishing to make sure that God had received my message. I then stood up and, immediately, my body began to react to my hard line stance with the Creator of the Universe. I was, after all, brought up to believe in Him as a real, living God—and now I was writing off thirty-eight years of my life as a "Christian," a life that at times had, indeed, experienced some elements of God but never seemed to produce a dividend.

My heart began pounding as my emotions churned wildly between frustration, anger, remorse, regret and even fear. I was now so worked up that I certainly couldn't go back to bed, and it was too early to go to work. As I stood there in the dark, numb with confusion, I saw my Bible lying on the end table and I began entertaining the thought of, Maybe one last time. I went through my three options—bed, work,

Bible—for another fifteen or twenty minutes, with bed and work having proven to be so unproductive for at least the last two weeks that they didn't seem to be much of an option for me.

I had no heart to pick up the Bible either because at that time it was nothing more than a useless rag to me. Furthermore, I had just finished making the decision to walk from God. After a tremendous internal battle, similar to all those traumatic altar calls I had endured in youth, I was feeling a strange internal tug to pick it up one more time. After allowing that feeling to well up in me to a point of beginning to feel urgent, I decided not to fight it off any longer so I picked it up, turned on the nearby lamp, opened it, and began to read.

To the Heart

What happened next is virtually unexplainable but, for the first time in my life, every word I read from the Bible suddenly skipped my brain and went directly to my heart. Instead of my reading, rereading, contemplating and then attempting to make the contemplation relevant for my life—every word, every thought, hit me straight in the heart. It seemed as if I were "mind-melding" with God, and yet my mind was not there to have to understand what I was reading. It felt as if someone had been holding my head under water and, just as I was about to die of suffocation, it was yanked out of the water and I was left to gasp for life-giving fresh air. My spiritually dried and parched body was now ingesting the "living water" that Jesus offered the woman at the well.

Without a warning, I exploded into tears. I hadn't cried in years, but now great sobs began to well up from deep within, as though my body was getting the chance to, finally, release years of pent-up praise.

With such expanding emotion welling up inside—emotion that had lain dormant for years, emotion that I had never even known existed in me—my mind began to analyze what was happening. The thought hit me: *What if this is a dirty trick played on me by Satan? What if this unbelievable, supernatural experience is something Satan designed and fabricated to jerk me around while I was at my lowest spiritual ebb?*

It was such a daunting thought amid such an incredible experience that I felt I had to respond by rebuking Satan in the name of Jesus. Having never done that (as far as I can remember) before, I nevertheless said, out loud: *In the name of Jesus and by the power in the blood He spilled on Calvary, get lost Satan, you and your evil forces have no right to mess with me during my time of connection with God.* I waited for a moment to see what was going to happen and then continued to read the Bible.

Nothing changed. I could still discern everything I was reading, and I was left with the bold conclusion that this experience truly was from God. God was speaking directly to me through the enduring words of Scripture! I spent the next two hours reading through tear-flooded eyes, with every word hitting me squarely in the chest while I uttered praise and thanksgiving. Before I knew it, I had to get ready for work.

With no other means of adequately expressing my feelings, I raised my hands in the air and, with one last burst of verbal praise and tears, I declared my allegiance to Jesus and recommitted my life to Him. I left that meeting with God, eternally changed. Though flying high, I couldn't help but wonder if this incredible experience would ever happen again, or was this simply a one-shot deal, with God letting me know, through an incredible miracle, that He was alive and well and that I should hang my spiritual life on that one experience alone. Was I simply supposed to quietly harbor the experience, as did Mary upon the visit from God's holy angel declaring the good news to her? Questions of what, how and why hit me with such rapidity that I was left virtually dysfunctional that day, in terms of focusing on my work.

My focus began to change to that of what is going to happen tomorrow morning when I get up again at 5:30 am. When the alarm went off the next morning, I didn't begrudgingly get out of bed but, rather, jumped out in eager anticipation. I definitely put a guard on my anticipation, because I didn't want to be disappointed if this truly had been a "once-in-a-lifetime" experience. I spent a little time praising God in prayer and then, guardedly, opened my Bible.

As I began to read, I immediately recognized that what I had hoped for, seemingly beyond hopes, again became a reality. God spoke to me in such clear and concise language that morning that it felt as if I were sharing His mind. The go-nowhere life I had become accustomed to living, I now realized, was never going to be the same, and all I could do was praise Jesus, who had revealed Himself to me in such a powerful manner.

The deal, in short—worked. And all I could think was, *OK, Jesus, now what?*

CHAPTER 4

KNOWING JESUS

O KAY, JESUS, NOW WHAT? FROM THAT DAY ON, MY LIFE began to change, radically. My reading of Scripture went from a mere intellectual attempt to understand teachings and doctrines into something else entirely, an experience that reached into my heart and soul. Through deep study of the Bible, as well as through prayer, I began to feel God's presence. I began to trust Him, to take Him at His Word as I never had before. I began to let go of self and to say, *You, Jesus, take control.*

I obtained great relief when I began to believe that I could "cast all my cares upon Him and lay all my burdens at His feet." I also began seeing my problems in proper perspective, that is, against the backdrop of God's sovereignty and providence.

Interestingly, I began to feel spiritually vulnerable, not my old independent self. I was more aware of my "filthy rags," which made Jesus' pure white robe of righteousness look that much more attractive. This realization led me to inherently crave more time with Him, of which time spent exposed more of my shortcomings, which pushed me to want more of Him, which in turn showed me even more of my own shortcomings, and so forth.

The fact of the matter was, I couldn't wait to get into the Bible every morning and, if I happened to miss it—my whole day felt incomplete and out of place. In the whole process, I was slowly dying to myself, while Jesus began living in and through me.

Salvation by Faith

I also noticed something else, something utterly crucial: For the first time in my life, I felt as though I didn't need to try to do good or to try to fulfill all the requirements I had grown up focusing on. Instead, I now fixated on Jesus, the Person, and what He had done for me at Calvary. By focusing on and being intrigued by His life, I became more and more aware of my sinful nature, especially pride. It very quickly led to awareness that, in terms of righteousness, I had nothing to offer God.

I was working from a position of complete emptiness and, as such, I began to truly understand Jesus' grace for the first time in my life. God accepted me, not because of anything I could do but only because of Jesus' righteousness covering me. This was the great gospel message that rings out all through the Bible and down through the Reformation to the present: *I am saved by Jesus, and what He has done for me, and not by my own works.*

What liberating news! The incredible part was, as a result of my time with Him in Bible study and prayer; He was beginning to transform my heart into one of dependence on Him. Jesus was simply giving me a new heart, one that started beating with purpose and relevance.

Love for the Lost

Another strange thing began to happen: A different kind of compassion for others started rising from deep within me. Yes, I had always harbored a subliminal dream of one day becoming biblically literate enough to share with and thus impact the lost in a big way, but I always had a wrong motive.

In reality, I wanted to look good, look like a hero of sorts. Self-centeredness or pride had so permeated my life that I could never trust the real motives for anything good that I did in the first place, especially for those who didn't deserve my kindness and those who, I coldly concluded, had chosen their own ill-destiny in life. If that destiny happened to be that of blowing their lives on self-destructive trivial pursuits such as partying, drinking, drugging, etcetera, I would simply say, *If you're dumb enough to blow your life like that, then you deserve to burn in hell, anyway.*

Now I suddenly wanted to share what I had so these people could have it too. The selfishness that had ruled my life for so many years was slowly eroding, and a softer side, one that yearned to see others benefit from a relationship with Jesus, emerged. I would look at people longer and ponder their lives and try to imagine the emptiness they must be feeling at not knowing what I was slowly discovering. My heart would then go out to them in a way that would make me feel lonely and maybe even a bit broken for them. I began yearning to share the good news with them, but at that point, I felt I was too much of a neophyte Christian to think that I could adequately represent my discoveries.

Questions that Need Answers

Amid all the change, a few things baffled me more than anything else, and no matter how hard I tried, I could not shake them. Indeed, they were haunting me with such penetration that I felt as if I couldn't proceed in my relationship with my Jesus until I was clear on two questions: *Why did I have to wait until I was thirty-eight years old before I was finally allowed a relationship with Jesus?* And, *Why did God seem to withdraw His presence from me when I was at my most vulnerable during my passionate, sixty day, pursuit of Him?* I mean—I was in the middle of a "do or die" deal with God, and I actually sensed that I was losing ground during my hour-a-day pursuit of Him. What was going on? Why did I have to experience such a dark separation before everything changed?

Thus, to seek for answers, I immediately turned my attention to studying the Bible with a new purpose, that of letting God answer my questions through the words He had delivered in it. One Bible reference, in particular, had hit me as a reality I wanted to have take place in my life. In John 14:26, I had read: "But the Helper, the Holy Spirit, whom the Father will send in My name, He will teach you all things, and bring to your remembrance all things that I said to you."

What impacted me most was the word all. This text hit me as the key to unlocking everything of importance in the Bible. Until then, I had taken to reading books written by human authors whenever I wanted to understand something. If I wanted to understand faith, I simply went to the Christian bookstore and purchased a book or books about faith, which I read with near-complete reliance on the author. After all, many were PhDs in theology or psychology. Also, the mere fact that someone engaged in the monumental task of writing a book made them seem credible in my mind, to the level of believing them to be the absolute authority on whatever subject they had written about.

The point? I had fallen into the trap of looking to others, rather than to the Holy Spirit and Bible study, for spiritual answers—and thus I was always living closer to the border of confusion than I was to confidently stand on solid biblical grounds. Now, though, I was going to rest my faith on the belief that the Holy Spirit would teach me, not just a few things but all things I needed to understand. I began to believe that there was only one way for the Holy Spirit to effectively teach me, and that was for me to make the Bible, and the Bible alone, the sole resource or textbook through which I would be taught.

In spite of the fact that many books are most certainly inspirational, I began to recognize that books were merely man's teachings of his finite discoveries. In contrast, the Bible, coupled with the Holy Spirit's discernment, were God's ways of speaking directly to me.

Never having been a great student, I felt challenged by the Bible itself, which is a gigantic work—made up of sixty-six mini-books written by dozens of authors over a period of more than a thousand years. Simply holding the massive textbook in my hands intimidated me at times; so forget about actually reading it. As I began to dig through the monumental work for answers to my questions, I would often despair and entertain the thought of simplifying the whole learning process by going back to my old ways of finding books written on a given topic by contemporary authors. Through it all though, I realized that deep understanding would come by no other way than by allowing my private tutor, the Holy Spirit, to teach me all things directly from the pages of the Holy Bible. Then, too, I had questions about how to read the Bible: *Do I begin reading in Genesis, the first book of the Bible, and then accept the fact that I will be forced to grind though the "begats" of Genesis 5 and other places in the Old Testament? Do I skip around the Bible, hoping that the Holy Spirit will miraculously lead me to the right page and reference related to a particular topic? Do I need a concordance? Do I need to understand Greek and Hebrew? What version of the Bible should I use? How am I supposed to link all the scattered texts on a given topic into one study so that it all makes sense in its proper context?*

And the biggest question, *Does it really even matter or make a difference if I learn more than I used to know. After all, more learning never seemed to improve my spiritual position in the past?*

Answers

In the end, I resolved to stick with my plan to use the Bible as my sole source of study, and then pray down the Holy Spirit to teach me, as promised by Jesus in John 16:7, 8—"Nevertheless I tell you the truth. It is to your advantage that I go away; for if I do not go away, the Helper will not come to you; but if I depart, I will send Him to you." "And when He has come, He will convict the world of sin, and of righteousness, and of judgment."

Now that I had decided to stick with the Bible alone, I began seeking the answers to the questions above. I desperately needed to understand why I struggled with so much dysfunctional pursuit for so many years, only now to have it all start sputtering to life. I needed to know what it was that I did or what it was that was so different this time that made the difference. In a way, I somehow felt that I had been cheated out of years of what I had always wanted.

I began fervently praying that Jesus would grant me the discernment and wisdom as well as the tutor He had promised He would give me, that of the Holy Spirit. With intense prayer, accompanied by my imagination in visualizing every thing I read, as well as a Strong's Concordance—I opened the Bible and began an intense search for an understanding of what it takes to have a relationship with Jesus.

Study was rough going, at first, and many times during those first few weeks I recognized that my progress was so falteringly slow and laborious that I again felt like packing it in and turning back to learning from the supposed experts. Amid the discouragement and the regular lapses in attention span during this pursuit, I became more and more fervent with Jesus to the point of actually demanding that He come through on His promise of giving me the Holy Spirit to teach me "all things."

At the same time, however, my study time for the first month did seem to be producing a few nuggets here and there, which I found greatly rewarding. I then discovered that, for every text that I found to be relevant and in context, I would be pointed in a new direction, and with the help of my concordance I would search for other texts with similar words and meanings. Slowly at first, and then with more frequency, I found myself moving beyond simply having a cash of random, if not disjointed texts on the subject and beginning to move into blocks of supportive thought.

Putting the Pieces Together

I began to realize that studying the Bible resembled putting a jigsaw puzzle together. In the beginning, I simply looked at the picture on the box of what my life now looked like with Jesus, and then I looked at the daunting pile of fragmented Bible texts that sat in front of me. I simply wanted to know what had happened that got me from where I was before to where I was today, in terms of my spiritual growth. I wanted to reconstruct the events of my life, only instead of simply looking at it as I would the picture on the box; I wanted to look at each biblical piece as they together formed the picture.

At first I simply shuffled through the texts, finding a piece here and a piece there that seemed to be similar in nature. Then, occasionally, I would experience the thrill of finding two pieces that actually fit together. This continued for some time until I could put small blocks together to create larger blocks. But, and here's the great point: these larger blocks actually displayed recognizable fragments of my life. As I began to see blocks of a picture forming, my excitement began to grow until my pursuit became passionately consuming. I found I could hardly walk away from my puzzle because I felt as if the next piece had to be only a few words away from the last one.

My process of discovery continued, for a few years actually, as I discovered what it takes to have a relationship with Jesus. What now drove my desire for discovery more than anything else was the fact that I began to see why, for the first time in my life, I had missed the mark for thirty-eight years and what it actually means to "give one's heart to the Lord."

Both my questions were, during this time, answered with one realization becoming very dominant: it is one thing to *know* a lot *about* someone; it is entirely another to *know* that individual *personally.* Just as I have read much about celebrities such as Princess Diana, and know enough about her life, to be able to share some facts with others, so I have always been able to present facts relating to God. But as I have never met Princess Diana in person, I had never met Jesus on a personal, one-to-one basis, either. In this context, head-knowledge about God was marginally OK for most of my life, but it was certainly far short of enough to impact my life.

Prior to my finding Jesus, when I was thirty-eight years old, my Christian life was nothing more than a game of *Trivial Pursuit,* complete with scribble pads and cheap pencils. Sure, I could discuss Bible-related issues, and could debate theology with the best of them, but all this did absolutely nothing for me in terms of true spirituality. My real message was always, *Look how learned I am in the Bible. With all the knowledge I have at my mind's fingertips, it can only be concluded that I must be engaged in a closer relationship with God than you are.* Unfortunately I had never really met the Master and, therefore, was only able to talk about Him without ever knowing Him personally, in the same way I could talk about Diana without ever knowing her well.

Thus, here lay the answer to my two questions. First, all those years of Christian roll-playing passed me by as spiritually irrelevant because all I had to rest my weary soul on was a cache of facts about God; I had never come to know Him for myself. Second, God had seemed to withdraw Himself from me at that time for two reasons. He knew that I both needed to be broken, humbled and brought to my knees in death-to-self before I could come to know Him. More importantly, I needed to understand what passionate pursuit of our Savior is all about, details to be revealed later.

The Knowledge of God

Thus, over a seemingly great period of time, my greatest need of understanding, that of what it actually took to have a dynamic relationship with Jesus was finally fulfilled by the teaching of the Holy Spirit. I now clearly understood that without a personal and intimate relationship with Jesus, fact-knowledge of Him as well as doctrinal understanding is of total irrelevance. Certainly, I was experiencing a personal transformation beyond my wildest imagination but of monumentally greater importance to me was that I had been led to now intellectually understand exactly what it was that I had gone through as well as led to clearly see just what it takes to have a dynamic, dividend-paying relationship with Jesus.

The Bible was so plain, so clear, that it baffled me why I had never heard the simple truth before. I felt cheated that I had lost thirty-eight years of potential relationship with a God I had always believed to be of reality but of whom I could never find a personal connection with. Why had all those preachers and teachers, I had so intently listened to as a young person chosen to deliver hell-fire and brimstone as well as works-oriented sermons instead of the simple beautiful truth of what it actually takes to have a relationship with Jesus? Was it because they didn't know themselves and thus could not offer that which they did not possess? Was it because they assumed everyone else already understood such basics and therefore moved on to feature the meatier doctrine-heavy topics?

Although I would like to know the answers to these questions, they are not for me to understand as all that matters is, I was led by the Holy Spirit to the discovery of just what it took, in my own life, to have an incredible, personal relationship with Jesus. I believe it is more appropriate to allow the personal testimonies of literally tens of thousands of people around the globe I have shared the simple truth with, through television, DVDs, preaching and one on one sharing, who have validated that message with praise to Jesus for their own personal discovery of Him.

You see, unknown to me at the time of my true conversion experience, I had actually gone through three steps or levels of involvement with Jesus that led to the relationship I had so yearned for my whole life.

I, therefore, offer through the rest of this book what I could label as, "Three Steps to a Dynamic Relationship With Jesus" that will—not *might*—lead to "Falling in Love With Jesus."

CHAPTER 5

THE FIRST STEP

I BEGIN WITH A CAVEAT. WE OFTEN LIKE TO PACKAGE OUR presentations or biblical discoveries in neat little compartmentalized boxes whereby we number things or outline them as though that is the one way God thinks or the only way things can take place. You know—"Twelve Steps to . . ." or "Seven Ways to . . ."

That might be fine for some topics but we can never hope to capture even a fragment of the ways and means of God in mere human terms or words, especially if we narrow the scope of God down to simplistic steps or numbers in an outline.

I believe we should not build, what I call, "bird houses for the Holy Spirit," in that we may come up with what sounds logical to us and then ask the Holy Spirit to inhabit our plan or understanding to the level of bringing it to fruition. Rather, we should be completely open to allowing the Holy Spirit, in each specific instance, to do what the Holy Spirit deems most fitting. Thus, it would be more appropriate for me to state that there are three biblically prescribed levels of enactment or engagement that must be present in order to possess a dynamic relationship with Jesus. How we will experience them is, of course, dependent upon our own circumstances but, in principle, these three steps have arisen from the Word of God as delivered by the Holy Spirit.

Admit You Have a Problem

Says the apostle Paul, "Examine yourselves as to whether you are in the faith. Test yourselves" (2 Corinthians 13:5). In essence, we are informed here that we are to take a serious look at our own spiritual lives, in evaluation of whether or not all is right between us and our Savior, Jesus.

It is obviously not enough to just go through life content that what we are spiritually experiencing is the epitome of what God wants with us and for us. We are, rather, to engage ourselves in deep spiritual self-analysis, looking for that little sin tendency here or that blatant iniquitous act or thought there and, then—do something about it.

When the text states we are to "examine" ourselves, the connotation should be that of a medical exam. As a doctor examines for physical aberrations, so we are to examine ourselves for spiritual ones, because it should be our perpetual concern to maintain spiritual progress. The important thing to focus on at this point is the fact that God expects us to take a careful look at our own lives in order to recognize our need of His grace.

Identify the Problem

The first action then, that needs to take place if you wish to pursue a dynamic relationship with Jesus, a relationship that goes beyond mere church-going, a relationship that is filled with power and action, is to acknowledge that quite possibly you have a problem that needs to be corrected. Acknowledgement that something is spiritually out of order or broken and needs to be fixed is a gigantic prerequisite to moving ahead in the pursuit of the kind of relationship that God expects one to have with His dear Son, Jesus. As a matter of supportive reference, the first step found in the renowned Twelve Steps program to recovery is acknowledging you have a problem that needs to be fixed.

To take the whole idea of acknowledgement a step further, the very essence of what Jesus' grace is all about is negated if there is not an understanding that a problem exists in the first place. Why would you need the grace of Jesus if everything were spiritually okay in your life? Where would the sense of urgency come from, that nagging feeling that "I must deal with this before it literally kills me," if it were not for an understanding that I do have a problem that, left unchecked, is going to lead me to eternal death? What would be the motivation to move beyond a state of limbo or the status quo and into a position of actually needing something as humanly undeserved as Divine grace?

There is no such thing as earning Jesus' Grace in the first place, as in and of itself; it exists as a freewill gift, motivated by unimaginable, unconditional love for lost humankind. There is also no such thing as needing Jesus' Grace if there is not an understanding that "I am a sinner who has a serious sin problem and as such am in dire need of something I don't deserve nor can I earn.

I have only one single option available to me and that is to accept the incomprehensible fact that the God who created me, loves me to such an extent that He hung on a cruel and demeaning cross two thousand years ago. There He died alone, separated from His dear Father because the shame of my sin hung so heavy on His innocent shoulders that He could not look anywhere but at the horrific filth He bore. Without that grace, even hope itself would elude me, to say nothing of tasting eternal life with the God of infinite love and compassion.

Ask Some Questions

But, you ask, *What if I don't see myself as having a spiritual problem? What if I am so convinced that Jesus' grace covers me as a sinner to the extent that I no longer feel the shame of my sin and I now live in such "joy of righteous feeling" that I really sense no need of further spiritual growth? What if I have found such "happiness" in religion that I am no longer aware of the fact that I wear filthy rags, but instead wear Jesus' righteousness to the extent that I stand perfect before God the Father, content that all has been taken care of on the very cross mentioned? Am I supposed to focus on my sins to the extent of living with its horror and as a result, live a life of debasement, one where I have no personal self-esteem?* And, *Are you expecting me to abandon the confidence that comes with my belief that I have been saved and as such have already been granted eternal life, from the date of my conversion?*

Obviously these kinds of questions subliminally reflect some commonly held theological beliefs, of which beliefs, I have, in the past, adhered to some of the same. Sure, most definitely we are saved by what Jesus has done for us, and we should have an assurance of Salvation, but the real question should loom, *Is there a possibility that our spiritual contentment is of such dominance that we no longer understand the ugly reality that we are, and will continue to be, sinners in desperate need of a Savior?* Could it be that we have become so self-righteous that sin appears to no longer be an issue for us to the level that we don't recognize the fact that we have a problem?

The problem is, such beliefs as "Don't worry, be happy! Jesus has already taken care of everything for you." That's called, "Once saved, always saved. In testimonial form, it goes like this: "I got saved in 1974, so from that point on, everything is fine with me and God, no matter what I do." Or as a revivalist preacher might put it: "Give your heart to the Lord; stand up for Him and be baptized." Or from the even less committed: "As long as you are a good person and go to church once in a while, everything will be fine between you and God." There are a myriad of other biblically ignorant belief systems as to what it takes to have a relationship with Jesus.

Why do I say them? Because the standard of spiritual experience observed within Christianity in developed, affluent countries such as the United States of America, Canada, Australia, New Zealand, and all parts of Europe, falls considerable short of the standard of experience set out in the Bible.

Looking at Christianity as a whole, I believe it must be stated that a real problem arises when we attempt to assess ourselves based on what we observe in Christianity as a whole. If we base the assessment of our own spiritual lives on what we observe through comparison to others, we are being extremely unwise according to Paul. In 2 Corinthians 10:12–14 he gives us a bold warning as to what we "dare" not do: "For we *dare* not make ourselves of the number, or compare ourselves with some that commend themselves: but they measuring themselves by themselves, and comparing themselves among themselves, are not wise. But we will not boast of things without our measure, but according to the measure of the rule which God hath distributed to us, a measure to reach even unto you. For we stretch not ourselves beyond our measure ..." (KJV, emphasis added).

Work to God's Standard

Why would Paul be warning us against this practice? It is because what we observe in others, as a standard of religious or spiritual comparator, will, in all cases, fall far short of the standard which God has established for us. Paul even adds to his warning, a solution, that of informing us of what standard we should measure ourselves or assess ourselves against. He states that it is to be "according to the measure of the rule which God hath distributed to us." What we are then left to discover is that of what is God's standard for a true Christian's life, that is, for those who give themselves completely to Him according to the three steps outlined in the following chapters.

Clearly, according to scripture anyhow, God's standard is to bring us joy, it is to bring us relevance, power, confidence, advantage and blessing. The Bible is full of God's promises of what He wishes to do for us, with us and through us if He becomes our sole master. It is therefore imperative that we measure ourselves against God-standards such as found in Mark 16:17, 18: "And these signs will follow those who believe: In My name they will cast out demons; they will speak with new tongues; they will take up serpents; and if they drink anything deadly, it will by no means hurt them; they will lay hands on the sick, and they will recover."

Upon reading this passage, the immediate question that begs to be asked is that of "Do you see this level of the miraculous taking place among the members of or within the churches around you today?" How regularly do you observe fellow church members casting out demons or miraculously communicating with others in foreign languages or laying hands on the sick and watching them be healed, all of which are the manifestations of God's standard by which we should measure ourselves?

The Bible gives more than a hint as to what it is, within the realm of the spiritual, that we are to focus on when comparing ourselves to God's standard. In Matthew 7:20 we are given a statement of fact as to what type of measure will expose whether or not we are truly in the light. "Therefore by their fruits you will know them." In other words, if you don't observe the things of Mark 16:17, 18 happening around you, then there is more than a good chance that your church's overall spirituality is in dire need of a spiritual tune-up, if not, an all out resurrection. It is a standard of comparison based solely on the output of your and my spiritual lives. If there does not exist some observable, physical outcome pouring out of our lives, then, according to this text, be rest assured that the output equals what is happening inside—obviously nothing spiritual could be happening inside in a life that is not producing Godly fruit.

To our understanding of God's standard of measure verses our humanly concocted way of comparing ourselves with other humans, Jesus, in His own words, reveals a level of measure beyond anything any Christian believer could probably even grasp, let alone comprehend. In John 14:12 we find the simple, yet shocking statement, "Most assuredly, I say to you, he who believes in Me, the works that I do he will do also; and greater works than these he will do, because I go to My Father."

To think for one moment that the level of fruit-bearing Jesus is actually expecting to be able to perform through the lives of those who consider themselves to be His followers is to be equal to or greater than that as found through His ministry here on Earth, should leave us with a very sick, sinking feeling. To observe in ones own life, a level of fruit-bearing above and beyond that which our very Savior experienced, places the bar so high that we should all find ourselves crashing to our knees in humble cries for His mercy. For most of my life I compared the level of my spiritual life with that of the fruit output I observed in my church and, to be deadly honest, I came away actually feeling spiritually normal or average.

Unfortunately for me though, and in direct contrast to the Biblical standard quoted above in Mark 16:17, 18, I was, in reality, comparing my spiritual life with that of a bunch of dead and rotting religious corpses and in doing so, found myself to be right in there with the rest of them. I now recognize, rather painfully, that in comparing my life with the Biblical standard of measure, my spiritual life, in reality, was and is a dead and rotting corpse against Jesus' life. I recognize that my clothing is comprised of nothing more than the "filthy rags" of Isaiah 64:6—"But we are all like an unclean thing, And all our righteousness's are like filthy rags." Fortunately for me, though, there exists other garments in which to cover my filth, that of the robe of Jesus' righteousness described a little further along in verse ten: "He has clothed me with the garments of salvation, He has covered me with the robe of *righteousness*" (emphasis added).

How then do we deal with the very real fact that there appears to be very few, if any, trees bearing fruit in the orchard of the church within developed countries? Jesus, after all, gave us a clear understanding of what is to happen to any branch, even a whole tree, that doesn't produce fruit: "A certain man had a fig tree planted in his vineyard, and he came seeking fruit on it and found none. Then he said to the keeper of his vineyard, 'Look, for three years I have come seeking fruit on this fig tree and find none. Cut it down; why does it use up the ground?'"

In addition, in the parable of the vine and branches of John 15:1–6, we observe a rather disconcerting outcome for such unproductive behavior: "I am the true vine, and My Father is the vinedresser. Every branch in Me that does not bear fruit He takes away; and every branch that bears fruit He prunes, that it may bear more fruit. . . . I am the vine, you are the branches. He who abides in Me, and I in him, bears much fruit; for without Me you can do nothing. If anyone does not abide in Me, he is cast out as a branch and is withered; and they gather them and throw them into the fire, and they are burned."

Clearly, if there is no good fruit growing from an ostensible Christian, in other words there are no miracles, no outward signs of productivity for God's Kingdom by way of seeking to save that which is lost, then those branches or trees will be cut down and discarded. The point I wish to make here is that if I conclude that what I see in my church is the extent to which, or the limitation of what we are to expect from God today, and then I go ahead and use what I observe in others as a means of spiritually evaluating myself, I will quickly find myself in a whole heap of trouble. To engage in this practice then becomes the epitome of endorsing a faulty standard of comparison. Fruitless branches in a church are destined to be cut off and burned in the junk pile of hell so to compare ourselves with branches that are to be destroyed, is to set our sights so low as to join the unrighteous in their dead-end fate.

On the other hand, the standard of comparison Jesus suggests we adopt, that of what He promised our lives would look like, is to be a measure that will be inherently anointed with experiences of the super-natural. So as not to leave us hanging or wondering what His standard may look like in a human life, Jesus gave us a most graphic record of example through the Bible book of Acts of the Apostles. There we find titillating stories of miracles beyond human comprehension: stories of healings; demons being cast out; thousands responding in commitment to the simple message delivered by followers such as Peter; the mere shadow of Peter healing; the scarf of Paul being taken to another location to be used in healing; as well as, unbelievably, people being raised from the dead. What are we to make of this Bible record?

Of relevant note is the fact that chronologically, these experiences took place at a point after Jesus' death, resurrection and ascension into Heaven. Interestingly, you and I are living post Jesus' death and resurrection as well. These amazing stories took place mostly at the hand of simple, untheologically educated people. Again, interestingly, I am a simple person of no formal theological education. Peter and many of the other disciples were crude at times, rude, and most definitely of the sinner type. How could I ignore the fact that I am like that as well? For all the similarities I have in common with the disciples, one of the big differences is Peter's seeming to think that what was going on around him, in terms of all the miracles, etcetera, was not considered strange or out of the ordinary for any Christian disciple of Jesus. Rather it was all in a normal day's work. This is evidenced by the fact that he got a little agitated at the people who were stunned and amazed at his and John's healing of the lame man at the temple gate, the one where Peter said, "Silver and gold have I none; but such as I have give I thee." Peter is actually puzzled as to why anyone would think this miracle was simply not normal, everyday Christian practice. We read Peter's response in Acts 3:12. "So when Peter saw it, he responded to the people: 'Men of Israel, why do you marvel at this? Or why look so intently at us, as though by our own power or godliness we had made this man walk?'"

Peter was here having a hard time understanding why anyone would be amazed at something so routine as a healing by a follower of Jesus. To Peter, this miracle was simply all in a normal day's work. I, on the other hand, am at such a level of unbelief as to consider the miracle virtually impossible to take place in my country, during my time in history.

Are we then simply left to use the book of Acts, with all its amazing stories, as a sort-of spiritual history book of bygone days–complete with experiences of such magnitude as will never be witnessed again? Is it simply fodder for contemplation as to how powerful God can be if and when He chooses to use that power? The disconcerting part of the acts of the book of Acts is that of the strong emphasis God made elsewhere in the Bible regarding the fact that He doesn't change. In Malachi 3:6 we read a bold statement of fact complete with who actually made the statement as well as their title. "For I am the LORD, I do not change." Also in the New Testament we read another related statement of fact. Hebrews 13:8 says, "Jesus Christ is the same yesterday, and to day, and for ever." The question that needs to be answered clearly, regarding the intent of these references, is that if Jesus isn't supposed to have changed, then why does He appear to change His spiritual emphasis from that which we read in the book of Acts to that which we never seem to be privy to witnessing today? Is it that we, today, are not capable of handling such levels of the miraculous? Is it that God's work needed to be conducted in a certain way at one time in history and entirely another way during our day?

For some reason, I get the feeling that the answer to the above questions is a resounding No! No, the book of Acts is not merely a reference book of amazing stories that are meant to simply display what God can do if He chooses to but now has chosen to remain physically silent. No, His seeming dead silence, in terms of openly manifesting Himself to the peoples of developed countries today, is not for the reason for our being incapable of handling such miraculous events. No, God would not need to change His methodology of exposing His great care and compassion for us through acts of power.

The mere fact that Jesus is the same yesterday, today and forever, including His desire to expose Himself to us, should open our eyes wide to the fact that there must exist a problem somewhere else. The fact of paramount importance to our very soul's salvation is to seek to understand why Jesus appears to have chosen to be deathly silent today. We must open our hearts wide to the discernment made available through the promised Holy Spirit to first understand whether or not there even exists a problem and then, if so, determine where the problems lie. Unless we pursue with all our hearts to make ourselves acutely aware of any potential issue that may have wedged itself between ourselves and our God and Creator, we will as a result be left openly wanting on the impending judgment day.

In offering input into the matter, I believe that anyone who has ever spent an ounce of time studying the Bible, complete with all the warnings delivered to the children of Israel by the prophets of the Old Testament, will quickly come to the conclusion that, yes, there definitely must exist a problem today and that problem has to exist with us human beings and not with God. I do not believe for one moment that God's silence from manifesting Himself to us today, to the level of what He did in the book of Acts, lies in Him having changed His agenda for reaching us with His hand of love and compassion.

One glance at God's modus operand exposed in John 3:16, should forever put to rest the fact that we, as human beings, must bare the fault of blame for God's seeming eerie silence. Quoting, "For God so loved the world, that he gave his only begotten Son, that whoever believes in him should not perish, but have everlasting life." This heart-wrenching record of God's undying agenda, that of loving to literal death each and every one of us, subliminally screams, *I would not have given up My dear Son for you if it were not for the fact that you have a problem and I desperately want to solve that problem for you.* What is left for us to understand, then, is not whether or not we have or are the problem, but rather what specifically is our problem.

Unfortunately, before we get involved in any self-analysis of potential problem, we must first raise a red flag of human behavior. We need to review the fact that human nature is such that it inherently displays a strong aversion to acknowledging that a problem or problems may exist in one's life. Whenever the topic of "you might have a problem" arises, a handy defense system called *denial* raises its ugly little head as a way of masking the reality that we may, in actual fact, have flawed or weak natures. We as humans have developed the innate skill of rationalization whereby we blot out negative thoughts and force ourselves to become content that all is fine and we are in need of no help, especially when it pertains to spiritual matters. In primarily developed countries, billions of dollars a year are spent on positive-thinking motivational programs that are designed to build self-esteem and an attitude of, *I can humanly rise above my problems*. People seek out the advise of gurus, psychics, spiritualists, religionists, or just about anyone who claims to be an authority on "how to unlock the power within."

Why then would anyone want to attempt to unearth an understanding that they have a problem? Who among the successful in life, if given the choice, chooses to dwell on a negative such as *I have a problem?*

As a rule, when God makes a clear statement regarding some important point or belief regarding us, we should never allow our own feelings or interpretation to overshadow those words, or for that matter we should never trust any thought we may humanly conjure up that may be in opposition to such topic. Although the following statement may sound like a sentence of run-on words and poor English, I find no other way to state it: *The real problem with the process of concluding we may have a problem is that we may not know we have a problem in which case we have a bigger problem than if we actually knew we had a problem.*

To apply an analogy to the statement, if I have cancer currently invading my body, does it not make sense to conclude that I have a bigger problem if I don't know I have the disease? Obviously, if I know I have cancer, I am in much better position for the simple and sole reason that if I know I have it, I can be proactive in taking steps to deal with it. If, on the other hand, I am unaware that it exists and therefore carry on life as usual, its lethal potential can continue to propagate and invade me to the point where it will become terminal.

To bring the point back to the spiritual application, simply put, there must first be an understanding that something needs to be fixed or changed before one applies any sort of solution. The problem arises when we, as humans, rationalize ourselves into believing that all is fine, and we are in need of nothing, especially when it pertains to spiritual matters. It is at this point that we must move outside our own rationalizations and rest on Jesus' assessment of our lives. What then does it mean to allow Jesus' assessment of our spiritual condition to be our guide?

It means this: take the Bible's advice as the analysis of who and what we are. A good starting point is to look at a piece of advice to find what not to do when it comes to the analysis of our own spirituality. In Proverbs 3:5 we read a very strong warning, one that is meant to wake us up to a potentially lethal thought process. It simply but powerfully states, "Lean not on your own understanding." Clearly, this is saying, "Just because some thought or emotion may feel right and it may even be supported by what seems to be relevant data, don't rest your belief on it." God is making it very plain to us that our human thought process is so flawed that it cannot be relied upon when dealing with spiritual self-analysis.

Assurance

At this juncture, I believe another very relevant question needs to be asked. How are we to deal with the seeming dichotomy of on the one hand understanding we have a serious sin problem and yet on the other hand being assured that we have salvation? If we are so bad, how can we know we are saved? Where's our hope?

For starters, assurance, in and of itself, should supersede doubt and therefore automatically lead to us feeling good about our spiritual selves, should it not? What is wrong with my accepting comfort from the fact that I can have an assurance of salvation based on Jesus' death for me on Calvary?

In one sense, these are valid questions and make good points. We must always rest our hope upon what Jesus has done for us; we must, in the end, know that our salvation is certain only in Him. But that wonderful truth should never cause us to rest contentedly on the side-lines of ministry, because if we truly are connected with Him, we will see more clearly than ever just how fallen we really are, and that will spur us on to seek Him even more urgently than we may right now. The point to consider is this, the day that we think that we "have arrived" spiritually is the day we can be sure that we are sadly deceived.

Nowhere can we see this imperative understanding illustrated more powerfully than that of listening to the warning words of the prophet Jeremiah. In Jeremiah 17:9 we read the ugly reality that "the heart is deceitful above all things and desperately wicked, who can know it?" Translation: "Your heart is a pathological liar, not only to others but to yourself and in addition to that it is not just wicked but, rather, desperately wicked and sinful in nature and the scary part of the whole assessment is, you don't know you have this problem."

As I've stated, the worst problem imaginable is one where you actually have a serious problem and don't know it, which inherently results in your doing nothing about it. Ignorance, in this case, isn't bliss. Rather, it's the kiss of death. God is informing us of what exactly we are dealing with when we consider the validity of an assessment based on a heart feeling. We simply cannot trust it because not only does it have a propensity to lie to us but also its entire motive is wicked and sin based. And if that isn't enough of a blast from on high, the scriptural reference continues with an even greater revelation of bad news. It would have been one thing if God had ended his evaluation of my heart saying, it is a wicked liar since I could then focus on taking what spiritual corrective measures I may, but unfortunately for me, it is entirely different when He gives me the real bad news, that I am not even remotely aware of the fact that I even have this problem. I am, in essence, brain-dead to the reality that a problem even exists.

According to this summation, if your heart is telling you that you are spiritually okay, then you must also understand that it is most definitely lying to you because you wouldn't know it in the first place anyhow. And furthermore, it is only through an understanding or knowledge that we have a problem that we would seek the solution of Jesus Christ and Him crucified.

It must be understood that this is a critical reality to understand. God has gone so far in His attempts to expose the danger of listening to our own self-assessments that He chose to leave us a mountain of records through the nearly perpetual warnings He delivered to His chosen people throughout the Old Testament. Virtually every one of the Old Testament prophet's sole mission was that of issuing a wake-up call to a wayward people who thought that all the religious rituals that they were engaging in, burnt offerings, feasts, sacrificing lambs, etcetera, would be plenty of effort to appease their Creator.

But, you may say, "That was then, but we are now." Fair enough, I don't believe one can find a better contemporary, if not futuristic, assessment in the Bible than that from the apocalyptic book of Revelation. Here we find God's definitive word of His people's spiritual condition. And what we can see is that of, in many ways, we are no different from the very people the Old Testament prophets were warning. Hence, the validity of their warnings is for us today. See what the New Testament says about us, the church known as *Laodicea*.

CHAPTER 6

THE LAODICEANS

REVELATION CHAPTERS TWO AND THREE PRESENT AN evaluation, as well as a warning, to different churches suffering different kinds of spiritual problems. The warning uses seven literal churches that existed back during the Old Testament Bible times, which were located in and around the Mediterranean. Each one of these churches suffered a different kind of problem. God used these churches to prophetically look ahead as a parallel to the actual evolution of the Christian church as it progressed from Jesus' time until the close of Earth's history. According to many theologians, each of the churches of John's day represented the chronological development of the Christian church, complete with the associated problem that particular church era experienced. Other theologians say that it wasn't so much a chronological parallel but rather an outline of different problems that different churches during different times in Earth's history would experience.

I lean toward a belief that each of these literal churches, with literal spiritual problems, was used to expose the problems experienced by the Christian church as it moved through history. Therefore the last of the seven churches is to us, who, obviously, live in the last days of earth's history, and so is of the utmost significance. In reality, it does not matter which belief system you endorse as long as you can recognize and associate the literal church problems back then with the problems our churches may be experiencing, today.

The Churches

Incidentally—or coincidently—the first literal church featured from the Mediterranean region during the writing of the book of Revelation also paralleled the problem experienced by the early Christian church, that is, the church that functioned immediately after the writing of the book of Revelation. We read in Revelation 2:4 that the church of Ephesus suffered from a spiritual problem, that it had left its "first love." In much the same way as some vibrant marriages lose its magic, this church also once had a vibrant relationship with God but, because of sin's intrusion, it had slowly lost its commitment to its true love, and separation was now lurking at the door. This was the shivering warning given from God to Ephesus, the first period of His church's post-New Testament existence.

In like manner to the church of Ephesus, each period of God's church from the New Testament beginning and onward was accurately assessed through prophecy before its time actually arrived. Smyrna and its evaluation is mentioned next, then Pergamos, Thyatira, Sardis and Philadelphia, followed by one more church, Laodicea, which represents the condition of God's church just before the end of the world. Based on biblical prophecy, there is left no stone of doubt unturned in warning us that we are now living in the last days of history. Thus, we must look at the cold and bold warning given to us, as that represented by the warning to Laodicea.

Laodicea

In Revelation 3:15, 16, God summarizes the condition of His church in Laodicea and how repulsive its nature is to Him. "I know your works, that you are neither cold nor hot. I could wish you were cold or hot. So then, because you are lukewarm, and neither cold nor hot, I will vomit you out of My mouth."

This is one of the starkest warnings in the Bible. Laodiceans are considered so distasteful to God that His response is to vomit, or "puke," them out of His mouth. This group of obvious church-going "Christians" literally turns God's stomach. If fact, God goes so far as to say, "I would rather that you be cold"—in other words, "far from me"—than the state where you are right now.

Upon the immediate reading of this God-response, we should find ourselves clamoring to understand just what is so distasteful to God. The answer can be found in the next verse, that of verse 17: "Because you say, 'I am rich, have become wealthy, and have need of nothing' and do not know that you are wretched, miserable, poor, blind, and naked."

We find here that there are two identifying conditions or problems that afflict this church of Laodicea, or the church that exists just before the end of times. They are as follows:

First, life is so easy that there is really no need for anything more including, and most significantly, the need of God. When it states that the members of this church era are "wealthy and have need of nothing," it is referring to the fact that they pretty much have all their basic needs met as well as more than what they really need. This would mean that they are blessed with the financial means to fulfill their core need of food, clothing, shelter and, to a lesser degree, things like transportation and maybe even some form of entertainment. If an individual has his or her basic survival needs met as well as many non-needs such as material-oriented objects like a bigger house than one actually really needs; fancier clothes than that which simply provide covering and warmth; a car or cars that provide options above and beyond the basic function of transporting you to your destination and then back again; furniture that goes beyond that of simply providing support while in the sitting position; computers beyond what is needed to conduct basic business; fancy dishes where the look is as important as the function; decorations and ornaments adorning both one's house as well as one's self; maybe something as extravagant as a pleasure boat of some sort; televisions, entertainment centers, video games, etcetera; then, put mildly, this person is extremely rich and certainly in true need of nothing more for physical needs.

The second and more dangerous symptom this group of so-called Christians suffers from is that they don't know they actually have a serious problem. They don't know that they are "wretched, and miserable, and poor, and blind, and naked." In fact, they actually think everything is fine in their spiritual lives. They go to church; they give offerings; they don't do this and they don't do that; they help those in need; they do many good things; some of the better ones even use their God-given talents to serve in positions of church office.

All in all they are wonderful people, at least in their own judgment.

Unfortunately, though, the warning states that they will be "puked" out of the mouth of Jesus. The real issue is they possess a heart that is "desperately wicked" and, worse yet, is lying to them—and they don't know it. As we saw already, logic alone will tell us that if we have a serious problem brewing within us, and we don't know it; we actually then have a bigger problem than if we did know it.

Many Will Say to Me . . .

One only need look at those self-deceived saints of Matthew 7:21–23, who stand at the pearly gates waiting for their admittance certificates to be handed to them, in order to understand that all may not be right when it comes right down to reward time. Verse 22: "Many will say to Me in that day, 'Lord, Lord, have we not prophesied in Your name, cast out demons in Your name, and done many wonders in Your name?'"

To be quite honest, these people appear to be way above and beyond anything I have yet to witness among any church-going Christians in any developed country today. They actually sound like those disciples we read about in the book of Acts, the ones whose action-filled lives leave us salivating in envy. Unfortunately, though, even this group of religious high-achievers seems to be encumbered with a fatal problem, in that the rest of the reference paints an unenviable picture of failure.

Quoting Matthew 7:21–23 in its entirety, we read: "Not everyone who says to Me, 'Lord, Lord,' shall enter the kingdom of heaven, but he who does the will of My Father in heaven. Many will say to Me in that day, 'Lord, Lord, have we not prophesied in Your name, cast out demons in Your name, and done many wonders in Your name?' And then I will declare to them, 'I never knew you; depart from Me, you who practice lawlessness!'"

How could Christians with such a spiritual resume be considered workers of "iniquity"? If people of that fruit-bearing caliber aren't going to make it, then hope is there for me, a person who can only dream of being involved with ministry to the level of "prophesying, casting out demons and doing many incredible works"?

A text like this should be considered a wake-up call to the fact that God has a standard and plan for us that so eclipses anything we could ever dream of, as to relegate us to the junk-heap of society's outcasts. It should very graphically indicate to us that most Christians today are nothing more than unfit gloaters of self-righteousness piety who won't even make it to the line-up for Heaven let alone actually make it to its gate. The Laodicean church-attendee has a numbness problem in that he or she has slowly drifted or digressed to a position of not being able to even remotely feel the bite of sin as it intrudes their lives.

Hypothermia and Laodicea

As an avid outdoorsman who is aware of the dangers of hypothermia, I have discovered a parallel between this subtle killer and that of the spiritual problem of Laodicea. If you understand how hypothermia works, meaning the potentially fatal condition of low body temperature, then it will be much easier for you to grasp what takes place in the Laodiceans.

It all begins when a warm body, which is meant to maintain a very specific core temperature of 98.6°F, finds itself surrounded by a substantially cooler environment. Since the body was created to generate its own heat through the burning of calories as one would burn wood in a stove, it is dependent on the decisional process of its mind to make sure that it is well insulated with clothing or covering when it is placed in a position to be exposed to the potentially cold world around it.

Sometimes there is a choice as to whether or not the human body is placed in a cold environment, such as is the case in hiking, skiing and swimming, while at other times the person is accidentally exposed to a cold through events such as falling through the ice on a lake, getting lost in the wilderness or breaking down in ones car during the severe winter.

Whatever the reason for being out in the cold, it is all about the temperature differential between the body's core temperature and the temperature impinging on it. In the case of hypothermia, the temperature differential is such whereby the cold outside the body wins out against or overcomes the warm temperature of the body to the level at which the body cools down to the point of no longer functioning, ultimately to the level of death itself.

The condition of hypothermia begins with the most vulnerable parts of the body first loosing the battle against the cold. Our fingertips and toes, which are the least insulated with skin, muscle and fat, as well as having the greatest surface area per unit of mass, inherently begin to feel the first twinges of cold's intrusion. Anyone who has ever been exposed to the extreme cold of winter, knows how physically painful the feeling can be at having their fingers chilled by the icy cold. In an attempt to warm them up, we most often use another part of the body to offset the cold. We tuck our hands under our armpits or cup our hands over our mouths and breath the warm air that is emitted from our lungs. As this is certainly an effective temporary means of attempting to overcome the pain of being exposed, it is most often impractical to continue this practice, as there are generally other things to contend with during this time of exposure to the hostile elements.

At the same time, although this feeling is unpleasant, those who have become accustomed to its intrusion don't generally panic over cold fingers or toes. Why?

First, their bodies are large in mass compared to the little digits out on its extremity, so why would they excessively worry as to whether or not their life is in danger simply because their little fingers and toes hurt from the cold? Second, the body has an interesting defense system. The same nerves that carry pain signals to the brain actually lose their ability to transport those signals when impinged upon by cold temperature. Their inability to pass along signals results in a feeling of numbness, which erases pain. Thus, the same cold that causes us such pain also erases that pain by numbing our nerve endings and, thus, offering relief.

First and foremost, we must understand that the condition of hypothermia is filled with warning signs of impending danger with each sign informing us that, if left unheeded, danger lurks around the corner. As mentioned above, the first things that generally happen when exposed to extreme cold is that the fingers and toes experience an aching pain from the bite of the cold temperature. This is a mini-warning sign that simply states, "You are in an environment that is hostile to you and this hostility is causing you to suffer." If the warning sign is left unheeded and the body is made to remain in the cold, the natural physiology of the body takes over, and the pain quickly dissipates and is overcome by numbness or a loss of sensation. Following numbness of fingers and toes is that of the cold penetrating deeper to that of the hands and feet. They also quickly encounter the warning sign of pain caused by the cold, but again, if left to remain exposed to the elements, they also soon become numb as well. Then it's the wrists and lower leg and so on and so on.

As one allows the extremities of the legs and arms to go through the bite of the cold stage and then the following numbness, there comes a point where the warm blood running out through the extremities and back again to be re-warmed, actually slowly begins to chill the body's core. But not to worry too much yet as the human body has the magnificent ability to create blood-warming heat through stoking the fire—burning more calories. Just as one would turn up the thermostat on the wall of your house to make the furnace kick in, so the body's natural thermostat is triggered which initiates the burning of more calories per minute than it is accustomed to while inhabiting a warm-surrounding environment.

Weird and wonderfully, the body turns up its heat production by way of triggering the physiological response of shivering. Simply put, shivering is the body's way of creating a surge in heat through micro-exercise. Just as your body gets warm to the point of sweating sometimes, during rigorous exercise, so your body creates more heat from mini-muscle contractions, which requires the burning of energy to, again, produce heat.

It must be stated that by now, in the process of falling to the icy grip of hypothermia, there have been several warning signs taking place, warnings that indicate that a problem is brewing. Failure to heed these warnings by protecting the body from further heat loss, can result in a catastrophic consequence, that of death itself. When the body begins to shiver in an attempt to equalize its heat loss, you are, at this point, being confronted with your strongest warning that a more serious problem is in progress. If you don't engage in some corrective measures such as putting on warmer clothing or simply getting out of the cold, your body will continue to shiver for a little while longer, but it will then undergo an involuntary assessment of the situation and conclude that it is better to conserve its remaining energy than attempt to continue to fight off the effects of the cold.

As the core temperature of a person's body continues to slowly drop, its shivering mechanism will eventually stop and the body will slip into preservation mode, that of just trying to survive. This is the last warning. Your body has informed you that it is no longer going to try to battle its temperature loss. You are now entering the most dangerous stage of survival because what happens next is hideous as well as merciful. Your mind now slowly begins to shut down to the point that you no longer possess a mental capacity in which to assess anything to do with your dangerous situation. When the mind numbs, you become content that everything is fine, and you then involuntarily begin doing the most damaging things possible. The amazing thing is that during this dementia stage, a person's mind actually begins believing that the body really feels warm. As a result, it no longer considers the external protection of clothes to be of much value, and the most hideous decisions are now made.

It must be plainly pointed out that at the point where the mind eventually looses its judgment or ability to assess the situation, only one hope is left for the victim of hypothermia and that is if some external element, namely a rescuer, is brought in to revive the person, otherwise death will be imminent.

Those trained in search and rescue are taught that if they find a hypothermic person who is in last stages of this condition, and if the rescuers do not have pre-warmed blankets or hot water bottles to place on the victim's body, they are to use their own body heat to attempt to warm the dying. By stripping both the victim and the rescuers of their clothes and then crawling into a sleeping bag or other protective covering, the body heat of the rescuer can then be used to heat the victim.

So many people who have been found dead from exposure, or hypothermia, have been found at the end of a trail of destruction. When tracking down those who have been lost in the woods or in a winter blizzard, searchers have reported similar, rather disturbing, events having taken place during a person's last moments or hours of life.

Many have reported finding a victim's gloves lying in the snow along a lost person's trail and then a little while later they may find a discarded hat, the most critical piece of protective clothing on the body. So many times a frozen body will be found to be wearing a warm coat but, for some bizarre and unfortunate reason, the jacket had been zipped opened at some point before death actually took place. The most interesting aspect of this gradual path to death is that contentment appears to be the last "state of being" for the victims before they finally succumb to death itself. It is said that the mind of a late stage hypothermic person actually tricks them into actually feeling like their bodies are really warm, and death comes with neutral feeling.

The Analogy

The point of this whole analogy is that the parallel between hypothermia and hypo-spirituality is so deadly close in symbolic symptom that it behooves us to look closely at each physiological hypothermic stage and then compare it with our spiritual lives.

The world we live in is a cold, dark place with sin rampant everywhere around us. We are nothing more than frail little bodies trying to survive the assault of a wicked and extremely deceptive antagonist. Satan will do anything and everything to slowly steal away our spiritual warmth. Hypo-spirituality definitely comes with a pattern of destruction through the slow and insidious process of eroding away the foundation on which and through which we live.

The first time we encounter an intrusive type sin from outside ourselves, it most definitely nips at our conscience in much the same way as the cold does to our fingers and toes. If we, as sheltered Christians, find ourselves in an environment where, for example, someone has the filthy habit of populating their speech with hard-core profanity, I will guarantee that we will find this behavior intrusive to the point of causing moral pain to even listen to it.

But interestingly, we need only to expose ourselves to such intrusive behavior for a few short days in a row, and the shock or pain of that exposure will slowly dissipate, and we will ultimately become numb to its bite in the same way our fingers, if left exposed to the cold, eventually turn numb as well. After our consciences go numb to the intrusive nature of someone else's profanity, and we continue to allow ourselves to be exposed to it, the day will come when we, in utter frustration over something, will utter our own profanity. Upon doing this, the cold of sin most definitely bites a little deeper; the pain moves closer to our soul's core. It is just like our hands and feet being exposed to the elements. They become painful, even though the fingers and toes are now numb. Sin's intrusion has gone a little deeper causing a new pain.

Interestingly though, one needs to use profanity only a few times and the shock and horror of our own self's sin will wear off and we will eventually become numb to that intrusion as well. Sin works exactly that way. It is ever a creeping compromise. The shock of a first encounter with any of Satan's intrusions, such as watching a murder or rape on a fictitious television show, or even the real life acts of war's destruction such as are regularly aired on the news, will hurt and cause moral pain; but if we continue to allow ourselves to be exposed to these intrusive elements, we will gradually callus over and become numb to its alien effects.

As sin gradually moves deeper into our soul's moral core, we begin to see a gradual drop in spiritual temperature, which drop will be so subtle as to most likely go completely unnoticed by our own self-assessment. If left to insidiously erode our spirituality, there will come a warning one day wherein we will wake up to the condition we are in and shudder or shiver at how far we have morally fallen. This is a bold warning by none other than the Holy Spirit, a warning meant to wake us up to the reality that we are drifting away from God and towards death itself. Unfortunately though, if we do not make a move to remove ourselves from the influence of sin's intrusion, even the still small voice of the Holy Spirit will eventually be frozen out, and we will be left in a state of late stage hypo-spirituality. The scariest part of the whole downward spiral into sin's degradation is that what goes next is our mind's ability to understand how dire our condition is. This is precisely what the church of Laodicea is all about.

Laodicean Christians are basically those who claim to have their spiritual act together. Unfortunately, though, they're suffering from late-stage hypo-spirituality:

▶ They have gone through all the warning signs of their extremities being nipped at by sin's intrusion and their consciences feeling the pain of that exposure.

▶ They have experienced the callusing or numbing effect of repeated exposure to sin's intrusion without withdrawing from its exposure.

▶ They have allowed sin's elements to slowly creep their way closer to the core of their beings with the result being their spiritual warmth or connection with Jesus being compromised and their passion for spiritual things having cooled.

▶ They have gone through the stage of waking up one morning to the recognition, through Holy Spirit prompting, that open sin was now comfortably a part of their lives.

▶ They realized that they were engaging in acts of sin today that they'd never have considered even a few months earlier, and in response, they shudder or shiver at how they've eroded spiritually.

▶ They have considered their errant ways, but it seemed too difficult to give them up and, after all, they rather enjoy what they are doing anyhow.

▶ They are almost oblivious to the fact that the shivering caused by sin-recognition has also subsided, and they again felt contented that all is okay, especially since Jesus' grace covers them anyhow.

Now, after having gone through all the early and later stages of the condition of hypo-spirituality, they are happy and contented. They feel warm and fuzzy among their churchgoing peers as they attend church, give tithes and offerings, take part in extra-curricular church activities, and so on. Overall, they feel everything is fine, especially since, when comparing themselves among themselves, they find themselves to be of average, if not, above average in spirituality. Sadly, oh so sadly, though, their spiritual core temperature has dipped so low that their mind's conscience is no longer capable of assessing their own condition, and they are now contentedly going to their eternal graves with a smile written on their frozen faces.

Step by Step

We must, then, heed the warning given to Laodicea. As the conscience is eroded and numbness, or an inability to feel or sense sin's assault, takes over, we are led to forget how far we have slipped in our closeness with God, and we begin to lose contact with the very source that warms us, that of a spiritual connectedness. Isaiah 59:1, 2 says, "Behold, the Lord's hand is not shortened, that it cannot save; nor His ear heavy, that it cannot hear. But your iniquities have separated you from your God; and your sins have hidden His face from you, So that He will not hear."

The problem never lies with God, but with us. Our sin-numbness is caused by nothing more than separation from God, which means we cannot perceive the still small voice of the Holy Spirit prompting us to cover up, cover up with the robe of Jesus' righteousness and let it warm your extremities.

Unfortunately, the whole sin problem plays itself out in a vicious cycle. Sin separates God's face from us; separation then makes it easier to sin the next time, and so we begin to gradually drift away from God, one step at a time. As we become more insensitive or oblivious to the feeling of sin, we slide to levels we once would have never imaged ourselves sinking to. But God is so gracious and caring that He will do everything in His power to attempt to wake us up to an understanding that we are traveling in a negative direction, one that leads us away from Him.

In the same way that our physical bodies react to the realization that our body temperature is cooling down, and it sends out a signal to begin shivering to restore heat, so God wakes our spiritual nature and allows it to shudder for a time so that we will recognize our morally degraded condition. This is our last perceived warning before we begin to sink into death's eternal grip. And, just as we find in hypothermia, so we find in hypo-spirituality, that without external warmth being applied, we will soon die of sin exposure.

However, if we do not place ourselves in a position to be rewarmed—rewarmed by an external source, that of a Savior waiting to draw us close for spiritual body heat–we will quickly find ourselves at the precise hypo-spiritual point that Jeremiah 17:9 refers to when it states, "you don't know you have a problem" as well as the problem with Laodiceans that of they "do not know that [they] are wretched, miserable, poor, blind, and naked."

Unfortunately for us, if unheeded, death's icy grip will eventually squeeze out our last spiritual heartbeat, and we will have slipped into death, completely content that everything was fine and, in fact, we may even have a smile frozen on our faces.

Wake Up!

Thus, we must wake up and be proactive. We need to make a U-turn based on the conclusion that there is something deviously wrong about the road we are on. Unfortunately, unless Laodiceans know that they have a problem, they will not seek a solution and, because Laodiceans don't know they have a problem, they will not find the resolve to change.

The solution then becomes, not what we think about ourselves, but rather about what God thinks of our condition. As Laodiceans, we need to turn to the Bible as a guide in helping us understand whether we have a problem to begin with. It is imperative, then, that we not listen to our own tainted assessments, but allow the Bible to offer God's assessment, so that we will allow Jesus' external warmth to revive us. We need to strip down to a level of shame for sins committed, and then allow Jesus' robe of righteousness to cover us and make us warm again.

We have to understand this classic Catch 22: If we don't know we have a problem, then how are we going to know we have a problem? The only out is to look beyond our own understanding to God's. We can't "lean unto [our] own understanding" because "your heart will lie to you." So what is a person to do?

CHAPTER 7

DENIERS OF THE POWER

THE CONCEPT OF SPIRITUAL HYPOTHERMIA SHOULD CAUSE all who claim to be Christian to take a serious look at his or her spiritual life. How well does that analogy apply to our own situation? Or do we not even see it? Romans 3:23 is a good starting point to show what kind of people need to hear that they may have a problem. It reads, *"all* have sinned, and fall short of the glory of God." *All,* as in *every* human being, with no exceptions.

God's assessment of us cuts even deeper with the blade of truth by describing what we are all about. Look at Romans 3:10–12: "There is none righteous, no, not one: There is none who understands, there is none who seeks after God. They have all turned aside; they have together become unprofitable; there is none who does good, no, not one."

How diffcrent is this assessment compared to what we are led to understand of Laodicean Christians. It is a chilling report card, especially for those of us who may be among mind-numb Laodicea. But maybe we need to let the truth hit us with a little pain; especially since there is a well-known, wise statement that says, "The truth hurts." If the truth is supposed to hurt, then what about the opposite of that summation? Could it be stated that if what we hear doesn't hurt, then maybe we don't have the truth in the first place?

Certainly we would like to think that there are some people in Christian society, particularly ourselves, who have figured things out and have their acts together to the point of being considered righteous, but then that would fly in the face of what appears to be a bold statement of fact, that of, "all have sinned."

God's assessment of what we are really like leaves little wiggle room. Every one of us is a sinner and, as such, are in dire need of something external to both wake us to the fact that we need warming as well as be allowed to deliver Divine body heat to our chilled souls. So what if we do buy into the fact that we last-day Christians are a bit numb to sin's intrusion and a short on understanding that we have a problem?

Again, we can't listen to our own lying heart, but rather we need to turn to the Bible to hear what God has to say about what that sinful nature looks like in a so-called Christian, so that we can attempt to identify it in ourselves. To begin with, we need to read what Paul, in 2 Timothy 3:1–4, has to say of a group of real bad sounding people: "In the last days . . . men will be lovers of themselves, lovers of money, boasters, proud, blasphemers, disobedient to parents, unthankful, unholy, unloving, unforgiving, slanderers, without self-control, brutal, despisers of good, traitors, headstrong, haughty, lovers of pleasure rather than lovers of God having a form of godliness but denying its power. And from such people turn away!" (2 Timothy 3:5).

Talk about an extensive list of bad things that bad people do. Paul did a masterful job of identifying characteristics found in those considered hard-core sinners. Certainly, this assessment must refer to those horrible people who live outside the doors of churches around the world—people who by nature are rotten to the core. Or does it?

Denying the Power

Interestingly, Paul prefaces his list with a historic time frame as to when we can expect these types of sinful characteristics to be most prevalent. He states that we can expect this type of sin-proliferation to manifest itself most boldly during the "last days" of earth's history.

That is, now! And why do I conclude thus? It is because anyone who has ever looked at the end time prophecies of Matthew 24, as well as those found in Daniel and Revelation, will no doubt know that we are currently living during Earth's closing days.

Since it is vitally important for us to make every effort to discover who Paul may have been writing about in 2 Timothy 3:1–4, we will continue reading on to see if there are any hints given as to whom this assessment may belong. As if to answer our question almost before we ask it, Paul relays the answer in verses 5 and 7, which state that this group of people have "a *form* of godliness, but deny its power" (emphasis added). Also, they are "always learning, and never able to come to the knowledge of the truth."

As a businessman working in the wider world, I spend my life associating with the unchurched and I do not see "a form of godliness" in those who don't pursue God nor do I observe them to be "ever learning" from the Bible. Thus, the identifying marks of these wicked-sounding people do not apply to the "lost" out in the world. So, then, to whom might it be referring?

In light of what the last-days, lukewarm Laodicean church is all about—those who Jesus will "spew" out—the identifying characteristics point to them. Church-going Laodiceans do have "a form of godliness" in that they attend church, do churchy things like socialize among themselves, give offerings, and engage in a myriad of other traditional, if not ritualistic, behaviors related to church affiliation.

They are also ever learning from the Bible through discussions, studies and reading books on Bible topics. The trouble is that through their lukewarmness they "deny the power" available through the outpouring of the Holy Spirit, and thus never wind up tapping into a genuine connection with their Lord and Savior Jesus. This same group of church-going people finds that they are never able to come to the knowledge of the truth. You see, there is obviously a giant difference between "learning" and "knowledge."

Learning is the cerebral intellectualism found in sitting around in Bible study classes at church and hashing and thrashing around topics, all the while looking for some tightly packaged definition of what they are discussing. When the definition is finally arrived at, everyone sits back in their church pews and with big, prideful smiles congratulate each other at having finally figured it all out. *Knowledge*, on the other hand, has everything to do with the base word found within it, that of, "to know", or in other words, "to possess an intimate relationship with." In the same way that you and I can garner many details about our favorite celebrity through the media, so we can garner many details about God through our church connections but when it really comes down to it, is anyone impressed, including God or the celebrity, if we've never met them personally and thus have no relationship with them?

God isn't interested in the intellectual conclusions we come to but, rather, the application of Biblical principles in our hearts. If we aren't living the gospel—that of "not I but Christ living in me" (Galatians 2:20)—then who cares what we may think we know. "Ever learning" without application to the level of "ever living" the Christian walk with Jesus is futile.

To sum up, Paul, in 2 Timothy 3:1–4, is talking about church-going Laodiceans. When he put together his comprehensive summary of all the characteristics of those who think everything is fine in their lives, he had "last days" Laodicean "Christians" on His mind. That is, the Bible is referring to you and me.

Whatever Happened to Miracles?

One glance through the book of the Acts of the Apostles, a book chalked full of other-world miracles at the hand of lowly uneducated Christ-followers, should suffice in letting us know that there must be a serious problem in and within Christian churches today.

To come to the fatalistic conclusion that God does not have the same agenda today as he did during the time of the early church, because we don't see the same level of miracles today, is to make God a liar based solely on what he had to say about His own unchangeable character. After all, as pointed out earlier, He left us both Old and New Testament references to this fact as can be found in the following texts: "For I am the Lord, I do not change" (Malachi 3:6) and, "Jesus Christ is the same yesterday, today, and forever" (Hebrews 13:8). Again, Mark 16:17, 18 should forever put to rest any doubt, no matter when in earth's short history, as to what God's standard is and what He fully expects to happen in those who closely follow His Son. "And these signs will follow those who believe: In My name they will cast out demons; they will speak with new tongues; they will take up serpents; and if they drink anything deadly, it will by no means hurt them; they will lay hands on the sick, and they will recover."

If you don't see these kind of amazing miracles happening in your church, then do not conclude that God has modified His agenda, rather, it is us who are responsible for the disconnect and thus the lack of fruit-bearing.

Self-assessments of the Righteous Kind

In this context, then, it is absolutely critical to "not lean on our own understanding" because that will be fatal in terms of where we will ultimately end up. God's assessment of our condition will obviously be in direct opposition to ours. There are many texts written by God-fearing, inspired individuals in both the Old and New Testaments that show a level of personal assessment that I have never perceived. Why is it that the mightiest of God's servants in the Bible had the most "loathsome" and self-debasing views of their own spiritual lives? For instance, Paul, the greatest evangelist ever, said this of himself: "O wretched man that I am! Who will deliver me from this body of death?" (Romans 7:24).

Of paramount significance to be found in this seemingly debasing statement of self-assessment, is that of how so totally opposite it is to that of the self-understanding Laodiceans possess. While Paul cries, "O *wretched* man that I am," Laodicean Christians "do not know that [they] you are *wretched*" (Revelation 3:17, emphasis added).

Why is it that a great Jesus-follower like Paul saw himself as wretched, while a Laodicean Christian doesn't know that they are? It is because sin numbs the senses, particularly our conscience, to the point where we cannot discern the fact that we have a serious problem.

King David, the person God labeled "a man after my own heart" (Acts 13:22), had this view of himself: "My iniquities have gone over my head; like a heavy burden they are too heavy for me. My wounds are foul and festering Because of my foolishness. I am troubled, I am bowed down greatly; I go mourning all the day long. For my loins are full of inflammation, And there is no soundness in my flesh. I am feeble and severely broken; I groan because of the turmoil of my heart" (Psalms 38:4–8).

How different an opinion this godly man has for himself in comparison to the self-righteous, self-sufficient attitude as exhibited by many "Christians" today. Job, the man God used to challenge the incessant accusations Satan perpetually hurdled against God's followers, had this to say of himself after he eventually discovered a different picture of God. "I have heard of You by the hearing of the ear, but now my eye sees You. Therefore I abhor myself, and repent in dust and ashes" (Job 42:5, 6).

Of note, when Job's eyes were opened to a new view of the God he served, his self-assessment also changed to that of abhorrence for his sinful-to-core state. Isaiah, a mighty prophet of God, did not have much better to say when talking of our human condition in a godly light. Isaiah 1:5, 6: "The whole head is sick, and the whole heart faints. From the sole of the foot even to the head, there is no soundness in it."

The list of similar quotations by the great spiritual leaders in the Bible goes on and on, all of which portray a completely different view of self-spirituality than what I possess in my life today. When we turn to the Bible and listen to those who had truly found knowledge, or a relationship with their God, we find a shift in view, or self-evaluation, that should not be casually overlooked. It is not that they had a poor self-image or low self-esteem but, rather, they saw what God saw in them because they were close enough to Him to allow His light to illuminate their defects.

Yet, in understanding that they had a problem, they rejoiced in the knowledge that there was such a thing called divine grace – the granting of undeserved compassion and favor. They stood before God, loathing themselves for their sins while praising Him that He was all merciful and infinitely compassionate when it came to understanding their propensity towards sin. Those who found a relationship with their Savior possessed an inner desire to live in tune with Him, even though they recognized they were completely unworthy of that relationship.

Personal Experience

As I diligently studied the topic of spiritual self-analysis through the Bible alone, I was left a little shaken in that if I, a Laodicean, was told by God that one of the signs of my state of being was that of I don't know I have a problem. My question then became, *How was I supposed to finally discover I* did *have a problem?*

So perplexed was I by this dilemma that I began fervently praying for the Holy Spirit to lead me to a divine means of actually assessing myself. It was of vital importance for me to understand how I was going to discover that I had a problem if I wasn't able to comprehend that on my own. Finally, after literally months of prayer and Bible study, God in His wonderful mercy gave me the discernment to grasp what it would take to let me see myself as I truly was, a lowly sinner in need of grace. I would once and for all have a means of assessing myself in a way where human justification could not enter in to taint my view of myself.

There were many texts that ultimately led me to this understanding but, probably, the more revealing one was found in Ezekiel 36:26–31. "I will give you a new heart and put a new spirit within you; I will take the heart of stone out of your flesh and give you a heart of flesh. I will put My Spirit within you and cause you to walk in My statutes, and you will *keep* My judgments and *do* them. Then you shall dwell in the land that I gave to your fathers; you shall be My people, and I will be your God. I will deliver you from all your uncleannesses. I will call for the grain and multiply it, and bring no famine upon you. And I will multiply the fruit of your trees and the increase of your fields, so that you need never again bear the reproach of famine among the nations. Then you will remember your evil ways and your deeds that were not good; and you will loathe yourselves in your own sight, for your iniquities and your abominations" (emphasis added).

So much of what I desired was exposed in this passage. First, within this passage is a hint as to what God wishes to do for me in my life. It simply states, "I will put my spirit within you, and cause you to walk in my statutes." What this is plainly saying is, "You don't have to attempt to somehow conjure up a way to want me. I will put that desire in your heart if you simply just allow me to do that for you."

What Ezekiel 36:26–31 was revealing to me was the fact that God desires to give me "a *new* heart" and a "*new* spirit," so that I might participate in a relationship with Him. But the part that hit me hardest was that of what would become of the view I had of myself, especially my self-righteousness? It states that my self-assessment would automatically change into the view that David, Job, Paul, and the rest of the great Bible characters had of themselves.

There, in verse 31, I found the key, the piece of the puzzle that I was looking for. It answered my question as to how I was to finally discover that I have a serious spiritual problem, namely that I actually don't think I have a problem. It states, "Then you will remember your evil ways and your deeds that were not good; and you will loathe yourselves in your own sight, for your iniquities and your abominations." In other words, once I am granted a new heart, only then "I will remember my own evil ways and my doings that were not good and I will loathe myself for my iniquities and abominations." In essence, what it is saying is I will never come to the conclusion that I have a problem until such time as I have allowed God to give me the new heart He so desires to impart to me. My responsibility in the whole relationship process is to pursue Jesus with a passion, let Him give me a new heart and then, and only then, I will have an understanding that I actually have a problem.

It seems so opposite in nature, that is to consider that it is only when I find a relationship with Jesus will I begin seeing my sin in its true light. One would think that the closer you get to Jesus, the more spiritual you become and thus the more spiritual you become, the less you would see of your sin. Quite the contrary, as we are informed that it is only when we find the relationship that we will begin to see our sin.

The point? Laodiceans obviously don't possess intimate relationships with Jesus, since they don't see that they are "wretched" sinners.

Interestingly, we discover that when King David said, "For my loins are full of inflammation, and there is no soundness in my flesh (Psalm 38:7), he manifested that which the prophet Ezekiel declared, that of "when, and only when, you get the new heart, then, and only then, will you loathe yourselves in your own sight." A gigantic cause and effect is clearly laid out here—that of, a *knowledge that we have a problem* will only come by way of moving beyond "learning about Jesus" to that of actually *knowing Him.* It is only at that point that we will ever have an understanding that we actually have a spiritual problem and it is only when we, like Paul—"O wretched man that I am" (Romans 7:24)—understand we have a problem that we could ever need or even appreciate the grace of Jesus.

Another Analogy

As a way of grasping this concept, look at it like this: Picture a very large warehouse with only a single man-door to its interior. With the lights on inside, you enter and are ushered to one end wall and told to stand there and face the wall opposite you. On that opposite wall is located a vanity mirror, one of those mirrors you may find in a prep room at a Hollywood-type talk show where guests get their makeup put on. It is one of those mirrors with many light bulbs positioned around the perimeter so that your face and clothes can be totally lit up. The lights around the mirror are off, and the lights in the warehouse are then turned off when the person who led you in leaves and shuts the sealed the door.

You now stand there in the oppressive darkness, so dark, in fact, that you begin to experience vertigo or the sense that you don't know which way is up. You put your hand in front of your face and the darkness is so dense and intruding that it is almost like you can feel the presence of your hand even though it doesn't touch you. As you stand there, you soon begin to get so disoriented that you aren't even sure whether you are even still standing upright. Your eyes strain to gather light to the point where your enlarged pupils nearly crowd out the colored part of your eyes. Now as you are beginning to panic because of both the weight of the darkness as well as the unfamiliarity of the building you are standing in, someone flips a switch and on the wall opposite you, the thirty, or so, light bulbs around the mirror turn on.

My question to you at this point is, *Can you see the light from the bulbs that were just turned on even though the vanity mirror is located a hundred feet from you?*

To ask such a no-brainer probably seems ridiculous in that the light would almost blind you as your pupils are so enlarged as they desperately seek to gather even any ray of light. In fact, so bright are they, that you are almost forced to look away as your eyes clamor to adjust to such contrast in the inky darkness surrounding it and you. Within a few seconds though, your eyes do adjust and you are left to fix your focus on the one thing, in such total darkness, that brings both orientation to your otherwise oppressive environment as well as comfort to your distressed mind.

Now another question: *Can you see yourself in the mirror that is surrounded by such incredible bright light bulbs?*

The answer is, no, you can't. Why?

It is because as bright as the light bulbs are to your eyes, you are standing at such a distance that they do not have the power to illuminate your body to such an extent that you can see your reflection in the mirror.

Jesus is that light in an otherwise totally dark world. And, just as we may struggle to find orientation in sin's dark world, when we observe Jesus, we are given a focus point as well as direction and orientation.

Unfortunately, though, if we observe Jesus at too far a distance, we will not be able to see our reflection in the mirror of His character. We can see the light but not our reflection in the mirror. Thus, Jesus beckons us, "Come to Me, all you who labor and are heavy laden, and I will give you rest" (Matthew 11:28, emphasis added). He wants us near Him so He invites us to walk towards Him. Now, we begin to make our way toward the light and the mirror contained within the perimeter of the light. When we first begin our journey towards the beckoning light, we cannot see ourselves in the mirror, as we are too far away to be illuminated by the lights surrounding it. But there does come a point whereby we get close enough for the light to illuminate us.

We then begin to see an outline of ourselves in the mirror, and we quickly become content that we are now standing within the reaches of Jesus glorious light and, as such, we stop right there. It feels good to see the light directly in front of us as well as we can look back to where we came from, as well as around us, and to just see shadows thrown by the light gives us a sense of orientation and comfort. We may choose to spend the rest of our lives at this distance, content that we have arrived and all is right.

But, instead, Jesus' never ending still small voice continues to beckon us to draw nearer. Let's suppose that we choose to respond to Jesus' invitation to draw nearer to Him. An interesting thing begins to take place. As we move closer to the lit mirror, the light's rays begin to illuminate us with greater and greater intensity and soon we can see in detail our eyes, nose and lips. At this point, we stand for a moment to just observe, and we more than likely conclude that we look pretty good.

Yet we still hear Him beckoning. As we move in closer and closer to the mirror, our view of ourselves begins to change. Why?

Because now the light is so illuminating, we begin to see things we hadn't noticed before. Those out of place hairs, clogged pores, and bags under our eyes all become exposed in the light of Jesus' glory, and we want to turn away. Even our clothes look somewhat tattered.

Now, and only now, do we recognize that we do not look as good as we always thought. Standing next to Jesus, we now fully recognize our need of Jesus' pure and undying grace. We begin desiring His perfect robe of righteousness, and the cover make-up that He so liberally offers. It is at this point of reference, standing right next to Jesus' dazzling light, that we are now made cognoscente of a brand new self assessment, that of "O wretched man [or woman] that I am."

The Bible gives us the essence of this analogy when, in 2 Corinthians 3:18, we are told: "But we all, with unveiled face, beholding as in a mirror the glory of the Lord, are being transformed into the same image from glory to glory, just as by the Spirit of the Lord." By recognizing that we are in need of a Savior to cover our blotches and sin-stains, we inherently become desperate for Him to cover our imperfections with His robe of righteousness and in doing so, we become a new creature in Him. That is precisely what Paul wrote about in 2 Corinthians 5:17, "Therefore, if anyone is in Christ, he is a new creation; old things have passed away; behold, all things have become new."

If on the other hand, we conclude that we don't look so good and as such simply decide to back away from the revealing mirror, rather than desiring a divine make-over promised by Jesus, we will soon find contentment again in the fact that all is fine in our spiritual lives and we will happily go on our merry way considering ourselves to be "good Christians." To walk away from the light— in an effort to hide from the details of our sin—inevitably leads us to forget about the fact that we are covered with nothing but "wounds, and bruises, and putrefying sores" (Isaiah 1:6) and we fall into the trap as exposed by James 1:23, 24, which reads, "For if anyone is a hearer of the word and not a doer, he is like a man observing his natural face in a mirror; for he observes himself, goes away, and immediately forgets what kind of man he was."

The strange mystery of sin is that it quickly and efficiently numbs our minds from the reality of our condition, and we forget the very thing that leads us to desire Jesus' Grace, that of acknowledging sin in our lives. It was through this recognition that Paul saw himself as the "wretched man" that he was. Paul stood so close to His master that the divine light of Jesus very clearly illuminated his every spot and stain and he was left to see himself as someone who desperately needed a Savior.

The Revelation

As the Holy Spirit lead me through my study of what it takes to have a dynamic relationship with Jesus and I was given the discernment to understand just what it was that was going on in my Laodicean life, I began to find this new-found information to be more than a bit disconcerting. On the one hand, I found God giving me a clear indication of what I am all about, a pathological sinner, but then on the other hand He was telling me that one of the symptoms of my sin-sickness was that of, I would be shackled with the inability to conclude that I even had a problem in the first place. This led me to get very fervent with the Holy Spirit through begging for some means of exposing my sins without my self-justification kicking in to soften the blow of reality. I needed something, maybe a text, maybe a self-question that would expose my sin-condition in such a way that I would crave the solution of Jesus' very Grace.

Graciously the Holy Spirit complied with my request and He began to lead me through a series of discovery texts, most significantly the Ezekiel 36 reference above, that eventually lead me to a means of self-analysis that was bullet proof against my ability to justify my own deviant sin-actions in life. It came by way of a question of self-analysis—a question that leaves no wiggle-room whatsoever in which to find a way to get around the reality of what I really am, that of a total sinner.

The Question

Here's a question to ask yourself: *Can I think of one other person in all of society in comparison to whom I am spiritually better?*

If my answer is, Yes, I can think of another person that I feel I am spiritually better than, then I am dealt the reality of my position in the great controversy between good and evil, that of, I have a serious sin problem. If, on the other hand, I am pursuing Jesus and my answer is, No, I can't think of anyone that I think I am spiritually better than, then praise God, because I am now seeing myself as who I really am that of, I am a filthy sinner who is in desperate need of a Savior. The understanding of the answer to this question is so profound that it actually allows us a glimpse into the great God-fearing minds of King Solomon, King David, Isaiah, Paul and others. You see great spiritual people like Paul saw themselves in a different light than I see myself.

Paul understood and was well aware of sin's role in his life that is why he cried out, "O wretched man that I am! who will deliver me from this body of death?" (Romans 7:24). I, on the other hand, a Laodicean Christian, don't know that I am "wretched, and miserable, and poor, and blind and naked" (Revelation 3:17). When I ask myself the spiritually revealing question above, my honest answer is usually, "Yes, I can think of many people I am spiritually better than." In fact, I can look at the exterior of a person and immediately conclude, "I am spiritually better than they are. After all, look at their trampy clothes, those tattoos, the lip-piercings and the can of beer in their hand."

Try as I might, I can't get over my spiritual superiority complex and, as such, am forced to attempt to endorse God's assessment of me, not my own. If I allow honesty to pervade, I simply cannot get around this question. It nails me with the reality of whom and what I am, a pathetic, out-of-control sinner who doesn't have a clue how bad I really am.

But how can we rely on some slick little question that someone seems to think is capable of exposing us as spiritual frauds? Why this question when there must be a ton of ways of measuring our spiritual condition and thus come to a legitimate conclusion on the matter?

It is because this question is impossible to get around, even when using human justification to cover for our sinful ways. It absolutely fits biblical test and as such should be taken deadly serious. To apply it, why not go to the spiritual giant, Paul and ask him a few questions?

"Paul, can you think of even one of Jesus' other disciples whom you think you might be spiritually better than?"

"No, I can't think of one other disciple that I am spiritually better than—'For I am the *least* of the apostles, who am not worthy to be called an apostle'" (1 Corinthians 15:9, emphasis added).

Moving to a second question, then, "Paul, can you think of one saint, or a Christian out there in the world that you think you are spiritually better than?"

Again, "No, in fact—'I am less than the least of all the saints'" (Ephesians 3:8). Paul is not satisfied with simply saying, "I am the *least* of all saints" adding the qualifier, "I am less than the least of all saints" (emphasis added).

And then Paul goes and sets a seemingly unattainable level of standard for spiritual self-awareness through the answer to the next question.

"Paul, can you think of one horrible sinner out there in the world that you think you are spiritually better than and, yes that includes hookers, drug dealers, rapists and pedophiles?"

His answer is a shocker, and we find it in (1 Timothy 1:15): "No," as a matter of sad fact—'Christ Jesus came into the world to save sinners; of whom *I am chief*'" (emphasis added).

Interestingly, Paul saw himself as the chief of all sinners, meaning, in his mind, no one was worse than he was and thus was in more need of Jesus' Grace. Paul obviously had something that I don't—something that led him to an entirely different self-assessment than I have of myself. How could it be that one of the great Bible characters couldn't see how "good" he really was?

Unfortunately, when I ask myself those kinds of questions, I am unable to offer an honest answer of "No" to anyone of them. Hidden deep inside my self-righteous soul I honestly think that I am spiritually better than a lot of, if not most, Christians, to say nothing of the "sinners" of the world. My "heart" is obviously in dire need of a spiritual tune up and that can only come by way of allowing Jesus full access to give me a heart-recreation or simply, the new heart talked of in Ezekiel 36.

Jesus' Input on the Question

In concert with the self-assessing question laid out above, Jesus sought to teach me the reality of my sinfulness through the delivery of a parable, a parable that supports the validity of the question. In Luke 18:9, He said: "Also He spoke this parable to some who trusted in themselves that they were righteous, and despised others."

In this verse, we find two means of identifying just whom this parable was targeting most and thus who needs to listen up and pay attention. First, the parable is targeting those who are inflicted with the sin-blight of self-righteousness and, secondly, those who are critical and judgmental of others. The trouble is, one of the inherent problems with self-righteous and judgmental people is that of the fact that they don't know they have this problem, otherwise they would shut their mouths and spend their "righteous" energies on correcting their own problems rather than attempting to fix those of others.

After identifying whom it is He is targeting in this parable, Jesus continues with His story: "Two men went up to the temple to pray, one a Pharisee and the other a tax collector. The Pharisee stood and prayed thus with himself, 'God, I thank You that I am not like other men—extortioners, unjust, adulterers, or even as this tax collector. I fast twice a week; I give tithes of all that I possess.' And the tax collector, standing afar off, would not so much as raise his eyes to heaven, but beat his breast, saying, 'God, be merciful to me a sinner!' I tell you, this man went down to his house justified rather than the other; for everyone who exalts himself will be humbled, and he who humbles himself will be exalted" (Luke 18:10–14).

Two men are featured in this parable, men from quite different backgrounds no doubt. What is most relevant in understanding, though, is not so much their varied backgrounds—one being rich and full of himself while the other more than likely poor and emotionally beat down—but how they view others in comparison with themselves. Let's ask them each a question.

"Mr. Pharisee, can you think of one other person in all of society that you think that you are spiritually better than?"

We don't even have to wait for his response as he has already answered it.

"Yes, of course I can think of many people I am spiritually better than, especially that loser publican cowering over their in the corner. What is he doing here defiling the temple anyhow? As I said, I am glad I am not like others are, sinners. I, after all, go to church, I even fast twice during the week as well and of course I give a generous tithe to the church."

The Pharisee had to look no further than everyone in his line of sight there in the temple. "God, I thank you, that I am not like other men."

It is now the turn of the publican to be asked the question: "Mr. Publican, can you think of one other person in all of society that you think you are spiritually better than?"

Not surprising, given his demeanor standing in the corner, his answer was quite different than that of the Pharisee.

"No, certainly there is no one as spiritually useless as I am. In fact, I guess I probably shouldn't even be in this beautiful place of worship in the first place."

The fact that the publican removed himself off to the side, where no one could see him disgracing the temple with his presence, tells us his answer. He is so aware of his sinful nature that he can't even lift his eyes towards Heaven. His disdain for the filth that clutters and mars his life makes him regret everything he ever did to hurt his Master. He has only one physical expression in which to expose his self-disdain: he "beat his breast" in agony.

In laying out these two character stories and their related answers to our question of assessment, Jesus gives us the answer as to who is connected to Him through grace and who is separated from Him through human pride and sin-adoration. "I tell you, this man [the publican who could answer "No" to the critical question] went down to his house justified rather than the other."

Self-righteousness in and of itself inherently leads those who practice it to believe that everything is okay between themselves and

God. In explanation, self-righteous people, by way of their focus on keeping record of the supposedly good things they are doing, find contentment in the knowledge that they are able to adhere to the little set of rules they have chosen as their standard of spiritual measure.

Consequently, they are prime candidates as people in desperate need of the "new heart" so that they can be given the vision to see themselves, as they truly are, pathological sinners in need of a Savior. The reality is, they need to move closer to Jesus so that His divine light can illuminate the real them, as is exposed through the filthy rags they are purported to wear as mentioned earlier. "But we are all like an unclean thing, and all our righteousnesses are like filthy rags; we all fade as a leaf, and our iniquities, like the wind, Have taken us away" (Isaiah 64:6).

Again, beautifully though, there is hope for "hopeless old me" in that there is another robe offered me that can and will cover my ugly self-righteous rags. We read about it in Isaiah 61:10 where it states, "I will greatly rejoice in the Lord, my soul shall be joyful in my God, for He has clothed me with the garments of salvation, He has covered me with the robe of righteousness, as a bridegroom decks himself with ornaments, and as a bride adorns herself with her jewels."

Another Contrast

To bring even more clarification to the two diametrically opposed viewpoints of those who consider themselves to be Christians, Jesus, in Matthew 25:31–46, features two groups of people. One group, the truly righteous, is completely unaware of the fact that they are even doing good. When Jesus said, "I was hungry and you gave Me food, I was thirsty and you gave Me drink, I was a stranger and you took Me in, I was naked and you clothed Me, I was sick and you visited Me, I was in prison and you came to Me" (verses 35, 36), they had no idea that they had even done these good things. That is why in verses 37 to 39 they respond with this: "Then the righteous will answer Him, saying, 'Lord, when did we see You hungry and feed You, or thirsty and give You drink? When did we see You a stranger and take You in, or naked and clothe You?'"

You see, those who were considered of the ranks of the righteous, were left to ask, "When did we do these things? I simply don't recall having ever been party to the deeds you talk of?" The righteous obviously had not been focusing on nor keeping record of their good deeds as they were oblivious to having ever served Jesus in the way that He claimed they had done. They had experienced the natural outcome of being connected with a compassionate Savior. Jesus touched people through them and because they were so connected to Him through relationship, they were completely unaware of the fact that they were doing extraordinarily good things. In simple, the righteous allowed the transplant of a "new heart" and as a result, their lives became a reflection of the heart surgeon.

The unrighteous, on the other hand, or more appropriately the group of self-righteous "Christians," were given the reason that they were not considered for eternal life. Verse 41 bares the ugly news for those who chose to allow the Laodicean state of unawareness permeate their lives. It rather coldly states, "Then He will also say to those on the left hand, Depart from Me, you cursed, into the everlasting fire prepared for the devil and his angels."

Jesus continues by allowing them an explanation as to why they were not chosen for eternal life. In verses 42 and 43, He states, "I was hungry and you gave Me no food; I was thirsty and you gave Me no drink; I was a stranger and you did not take Me in, naked and you did not clothe Me, sick and in prison and you did not visit Me."

The underlying issue to the very serious problem inflicting the unrighteous can be found in the response given by them to Jesus. In verse 44 we read, "Then they also will answer Him, saying, Lord, when did we see You hungry or thirsty or a stranger or naked or sick or in prison, and did not minister to You?"

The key statement here that differentiates the unrighteous from the righteous is that of the unrighteous ask, "When didn't we minister unto you?" In other words they were basically saying, "All along we have been doing good deeds as well as keeping track of them so how is possible that we failed to do something good for you, Jesus and not have remembered it?"

In comparing the two groups, the unrighteous, upon receiving the curse of death, respond differently. "We don't recall having not done these things" simply because they were focused on record keeping, and in doing so, they missed the spirit of doing what really mattered. The unrighteous suffered from the problem of lukewarmness and didn't know they had a problem. They were into the comparison game, where they would look at those around them and assess themselves by way of the level of righteousness they saw in others, and as long as they were above average in perceived "goodness" they were content that all was well in their spiritual journeys.

CHAPTER 8

COMPARISONS

A S A STATEMENT OF FACT, THE FATAL DELUSION OF Laodicean "Christians" is that they think that they are doing well on their spiritual journey when, in fact, they are on the road to perdition. They don't change their floundering ways. What they don't realize is that comparing themselves with others is like Al Capone, the renowned Mafia mob boss, comparing himself to someone like Hitler, and thinking: *Hey, even though I am considered by some to be a hard-core criminal with bootlegging, murder and extortion featured on my resume, I am really not all that bad, at least compared to Hitler.*

The real issue is that Laodiceans are notoriously associated with comparing themselves with others. Since, overall, they are "rich and in need of nothing," one of the general characteristics of that lifestyle is they are caught up in the very comparison game that drives materialism. They feel it is vital to keep up with the Jones. *I really need a nicer car or bigger house because my friends have that, and in addition to getting more attention than I do with what they drive or with what they live in, they seem to be happier with life than I am.*

As briefly outlined in Chapter Five, Paul warns us against the comparison game, especially when it pertains to spiritual things. In 2 Corinthians 10:12–16, he goes so far as to say "we dare not" engage in this practice, as it is "not wise" to do so. You see, he's saying that if you use your fellow church member's level of spirituality as the standard by which you measure your own spiritual performance, then you are going to, in all cases, fall radically short of the level of what God's plan or intention is for your life. Paul goes on in verse 13 to say that we must use God's established level of expectation as a means of measuring ourselves, according to what He has exposed as His standard.

Just what He has exposed as His intentions for our lives can be found through the example of observing every Godly person who is featured in the Bible.

Again, Mark 16:17, 18 is just one mind-boggling example of what we should expect to be the fruit of our lives if we choose to give ourselves fully over to Jesus. This particular example of what we should be measuring ourselves against should, expectantly, exceed anything most of us could, even in our wildest moments of imaginative thought, ever comprehend.

It states, "And these signs will follow those who believe: in My name they will cast out demons; they will speak with new tongues; they will take up serpents; and if they drink anything deadly, it will by no means hurt them; they will lay hands on the sick, and they will recover."

Deadly Drinks?

Let me ask, how many of you church-going Christians have pretty much grown accustomed to regularly seeing demons cast out during your church and prayer meeting services? Or how about having foreigners who don't speak your language visit your church and you walk away fully blessed by understanding every word delivered during your service? How about having no fear whatsoever of poisonous snakes, simply because you know that you and your fellow church members have a divine immunity towards their deadly venom? Anyone interested in having a cold drink of arsenic-laced punch? No worries. How regularly do you witness terminally ill people walking into your church and by the end of the service, jumping up and down accompanied by shouts of praise because they were healed? Are these types of earth-shattering signs becoming ho-hum to you because they are standard practice during your church services?

This may sound a little blunt or maybe even harsh, but the reality is, if we don't see these kinds of signs or manifestations surrounding our personal or church lives, then quite frankly, we should be shaking in our boots as the conclusion should be made that there is a big problem somewhere.

The Acts in "Acts"

When's the last time you read the book of Acts and didn't walk away feeling at least a twinge of disillusionment? Disillusioned because when comparing your personal and/or church lives with that of the experiences of the early church, you feel more than a little cheated at having been born during a time in Earth's history when it seems as though God has chosen to have a quiet time away from sensational visible action. After all, to read in Acts 2:2, 3 that "suddenly there came a sound from heaven, as of a rushing mighty wind, and it filled the whole house where they were sitting. Then there appeared to them divided tongues, as of fire, and one sat upon each of them"—and then to be almost forced to take a caffeine pill in order to make it through a boring church service, kind of leaves one more than a little disenchanted with what we laboriously experience today.

And to continue, Acts 2:4–12 states: "And they were all filled with the Holy Spirit and began to speak with other tongues, as the Spirit gave them utterance. And there were dwelling in Jerusalem Jews, devout men, from every nation under heaven. And when this sound occurred, the multitude came together, and were confused, because everyone heard them speak in his own language. Then they were all amazed and marveled, saying to one another, Look, are not all these who speak Galileans? And how is it that we hear, each in our own language in which we were born? Parthians and Medes and Elamites, those dwelling in Mesopotamia, Judea and Cappadocia, Pontus and Asia, Phrygia and Pamphylia, Egypt and the parts of Libya adjoining Cyrene, visitors from Rome, both Jews and proselytes, Cretans and Arabs—we hear them speaking in our own tongues the wonderful works of God. So they were all amazed and perplexed, saying to one another, 'Whatever could this mean?'"

Do you recall hearing about this as one of the signs of Mark 16:17, 18? If we race through the book of Acts just picking up a few of the highlights, we had better hope that we experience at least a little feeling of contemporary inadequacy, as to not feel such could very well indicate that quite possibly we have gone too far down the road of hypo-spirituality to even be revivable!

As proof of what God's engaged church looks like compared to ours of today, look at the following:

▶ **Acts 2:41:** "Then those who gladly received his word were baptized; and that day about three thousand souls were added to them."

▶ **Acts 4:4:** "However, many of those who heard the word believed; and the number of the men came to be about five thousand."

Has anyone seen that level of evangelism around their church lately, especially through the preaching of one of your lay people? Please!

▶ **Acts 5:14–16:** "And believers were increasingly added to the Lord, multitudes of both men and women, so that they brought the sick out into the streets and laid them on beds and couches, that at least the shadow of Peter passing by might fall on some of them. Also a multitude gathered from the surrounding cities to Jerusalem, bringing sick people and those who were tormented by unclean spirits, and they were all healed."

Imagine witnessing even a couple of people healed by the laying on of hands, let alone observing someone's mere shadow healing scores of people.

▶ **Acts 9:36–40:** "At Joppa there was a certain disciple named Tabitha, which is translated Dorcas. This woman was full of good works and charitable deeds which she did. But it happened in those days that she became sick and died. When they had washed her, they laid her in an upper room. And since Lydda was near Joppa, and the disciples had heard that Peter was there, they sent two men to him, imploring him not to delay in coming to them. Then Peter arose and went with them. When he had come, they brought him to the upper room. And all the widows stood by him weeping, showing the tunics and garments which Dorcas had made while she was with them. But Peter put them all out, and knelt down and prayed. And turning to the body he said, 'Tabitha, arise.' And she opened her eyes, and when she saw Peter she sat up."

Or, what do we do with this mind-blowing experience?

▶ **Acts 19:11, 12:** "God worked unusual miracles by the hands of Paul, so that even handkerchiefs . . . were brought from his body to the sick, and the diseases left them and the evil spirits went out of them."

I have heard of cases of intercessory prayer working before, but I can't recall ever having heard of the intercessory use of clothing to heal and cast out demons in absentia.

Which Standard?

The point of it all is this: There are two distinct standards by which we can compare our spiritual selves in an attempt to determine if all is right between us and our God. Depending on which one we choose, we will either contentedly sit back and enjoy the earthly ride, or we will sit up, take notice and get proactive about attempting to understand that we do have a problem and then to determine what the problem is.

You see, what we have just finished overviewing in the book of Acts is, according to Peter, nothing out of an ordinary day's work for Jesus' followers. What does that mean? Look at Acts 3:2–8. What happened here?

"And a certain man lame from his mother's womb was carried, whom they laid daily at the gate of the temple which is called Beautiful, to ask alms from those who entered the temple; who, seeing Peter and John about to go into the temple, asked for alms. And fixing his eyes on him, with John, Peter said, 'Look at us.' So he gave them his attention, expecting to receive something from them. Then Peter said, 'Silver and gold I do not have, but what I do have I give you: In the name of Jesus Christ of Nazareth, rise up and walk.' And he took him by the right hand and lifted him up, and immediately his feet and anklebones received strength. So he, leaping up, stood and walked and entered the temple with them—walking, leaping, and praising God."

In Acts 4:22 we are told that this man was older than forty years of age. This then means, that this same man would have been there begging at the entrance gate of the temple during the time Jesus frequented the temple. Thus, this beggar had to wait until a later date to receive the gift of healing. It would appear that Jesus probably ignored the man so that the impact of his healing would bring greater glory to God at a later date.

Indeed, people were amazed by the healings. Verses nine to eleven attest to the obvious: "All the people saw him walking and praising God. Then they knew that it was he who sat begging alms at the Beautiful Gate of the temple; and they were filled with wonder and amazement at what had happened to him. Now as the lame man who was healed held on to Peter and John, all the people ran together to them in the porch which is called Solomon's, greatly amazed."

What is of greater interest, though, is not that everyone was amazed at the miracle but rather Peter's response to their amazement. In Acts 3:12 we read, "When Peter saw it, he responded to the people: 'Men of Israel, why do you marvel at this?'"

Peter was more amazed at everyone else's amazement over the miracle and, therefore, thought it necessary to question their reaction.

What Peter said here in street language is simply: "I can't understand, for the life of me, why you guys are blown away by this act. This is nothing. If you have any belief or faith at all, you would consider this healing to be of the level of the mundane, everyday occurrence. I am, quite frankly, amazed that you would be amazed by it."

For Peter, faith in the power and understanding of God's agenda was so firm that he simply took it for granted that this level of sign or miraculous occurrence would be considered an everyday event, rather than something to go "wow" over.

The Contrast

When we glance around at ourselves today, bound in Laodicean chains, we see nothing spectacular taking place because, quite frankly, there is neither an anticipation that something should be happening nor an expectation of it either. We think that to hear the odd story of a miracle coming out of some foreign, third-world country at the hand of some totally dedicated-to-Jesus missionary is as good as it gets here on Earth today. We are left to either endorse the subliminal belief that what we see is what we get; in other words, we simply conclude that we must be living the epitome of what God has planned for us today, or we gradually drift away from God to the level of simply not caring. What we fail to conclude, unfortunately, is that there must exist a huge problem somewhere, with the problem quite possibly surrounding us and not God.

If we would only focus on and attempt to comprehend what Hebrews 13:8 states—that "Jesus Christ is the same yesterday, today, and forever" as well as Malachi 3:6—"I am the LORD, I do not change"—we would quickly conclude that the plan God has in store for us is virtually outside of the realm of what we can even comprehend. If God doesn't nor hasn't changed, then one should fully expect to witness, today, the level of the miraculous as was found in Jesus' ministry as well as in the book of Acts. Simply put, if we are not observing that level of the miraculous today, then we must conclude that the problem clearly lies with us and not with our unchangeable God.

One need only look at Matthew 7:21–23 and the sad scenario of many who stand at the very gates of Heaven—in eager anticipation of receiving their citizenship papers to paradise, to understand there exists a potential problem that all may not be as right as we think between us and God. The reference rather shockingly states, "Not everyone who says to Me, 'Lord, Lord,' shall enter the kingdom of heaven, but he who does the will of My Father in heaven. Many will say to Me in that day, 'Lord, Lord, have we not prophesied in Your name, cast out demons in Your name, and done many wonders in Your name?' And then I will declare to them, 'I never knew you; depart from Me, you who practice lawlessness!'"

What can we say when we read of people at this level of seemingly righteous achievement, not only being turned away at the very gates of Heaven, but being told that they are "workers of iniquity?" These people—people we would quickly conclude must be of the level of pillars-of-the-church types—have prophesied in God's name; they have cast out demons; they have done many incredibly wonderful works and yet even at their lofty level of seeming spirituality, they are met with this message. "I am sorry but I don't believe we've met; you who are so full of iniquitous works."

I do not, for one second, believe that Jesus offered up this scenario with the intent of leaving us to believe that the pursuit of Him is to be considered an arduous task with the reward of eternal life seemingly elusive, but rather, it is there to expose to us that our self-assessment may be faulty to the level of being fatal. We must wake up to the fact that quite possibly, Satan has numbed us with hypo-spirituality to such an extent that we are left to believe that all is right between ourselves and God, and that merely putting in "church-time" here on earth is good enough to earn God's Grace.

It is imperative to look at Paul's self-analysis, that being, "O wretched man that I am," and wake up to the fact that if we think any better of ourselves than that, then we must conclude that we're possibly dying a slow, suffocating death devoid of life-giving spiritual oxygen provided by our Savior, Christ. We must ask ourselves, Can I think of one other person in all of society that I think I am spiritually better than? then answer honestly. If our answer is Yes, I can think of a person I am spiritually better than, then we must get on our knees and passionately pursue a relationship with Jesus, so that the bright light of connection with Him will clearly reveal the filthy rags of righteousness we wear. If we don't see the "rags," then we're not going to ever need or want the robe, that is to say the pure white, unblemished robe of Jesus' righteousness.

To summarize, as Romans 6:23 states, "The wages of sin is death, but the gift of God is eternal life in Christ Jesus our Lord." It is this that should motivate us to move from step one, that of understanding we have a problem that needs to be fixed, to the next step of finding and possessing a dynamic relationship with our Lord.

CHAPTER 9

THE SEEKERS

O NCE WE HAVE COME TO GRIPS WITH THE HUGELY IMPOR-
tant fact that it really doesn't matter what our own wicked
and deceitful heart tells us, in terms of whether or not we
may feel content with our spiritual lives, the ugly reality of it all is
simply this: we most definitely do have a sin problem and, as such, we
are in desperate need of a solution. Unfortunately though, finding a
meaningful solution is obviously not as easy as one would think. If it
were that easy, then one would fully expect to observe the Christian
church in developed countries being completely on fire for Jesus.

There would be no lukewarm, go-through-the-motions trivial
pursuit as is near universally the case in Christianity today, but rather
there would be a mass-movement of red-hot revival within the
church with that movement then being contagiously spread outside
the church into the ranks of the post-modern secular. Jesus, as was
the case two thousand years ago, would again be the predominant
world headline. Of course there would be massive contention and
controversy over His name and yes, His followers would be persecuted

for their stand; history does repeat itself you know. One would even find a whole host of church leaders of every denomination trying to curb the movement as the revival would be well out of their control due to the amazing things happening at the hand of lowly, religiously-uneducated, common people.

If and/or when Jesus is eventually brought to the very center of people's lives, to the center of their homes, churches, and eventually society itself, the world will once again be thrown into a conundrum. So great will be the unmistakable presence of a divine, supernatural power that every person alive will be forced to join either one side or the other. There, unmistakably, will be only two poles in which to gravitate to—that of either good or evil. In the great judgment day there will be no middle-of-the-road lukewarm people or churches being admitted to Heaven—No, they will have been spewed out of the mouth of God long before. Thus, there will be only one state left in which to belong, either with the hot or with the cold.

Unfortunately though, for those lukewarm Christians who simply go through life content that all is fine between them and God, their lives will ultimately be considered more a detriment than an asset to God. If the banner of Christianity is proudly flown over their heads, and there exists no Holy Spirit-driven output from their lives, the world will be left to conclude that the supposed God of Heaven is as dull as the life of the Christian pronouncing his or her verbal allegiance. Simply put, if Christianity, as a whole, is not seeing a mass-movement of lost people yearning for what they have, a real-life, fruit producing relationship with a divine being, then quite frankly they probably don't have what they think they have. The fact is fruit grows in abundance only on the branch that is firmly connected to the vine. That is why Jesus gave us the parable of the vines and branches in John 15.

Vines and Branches

In John 15:5–7, He lays out the cold hard facts related directly to us, proclaimed Christians. Jesus states, "I am the vine, you are the branches. He who abides in Me, and I in him, bears much fruit; for without Me you can do nothing. If anyone does not abide in Me, he is cast out as a branch and is withered; and they gather them and throw them into the fire, and they are burned. If you abide in Me, and My words abide in you, you will ask what you desire, and it shall be done for you."

So much valuable information with so much cause and effect is laid out here that it behooves us to break it down a bit so that it can be applied to the state of Christian Laodicea. Of course it is easy to grasp the concept that Jesus is the vine to which we, the branches, are lovingly attached. A little more illusive in understanding is that of one simple problem; just because it may look like the branch is attached to the vine, does not necessarily mean it is receiving life-giving, fruit-supporting "living water." The reference clearly states two realities that should expose to our minds just what, exactly, Jesus is intending for us to understand.

Number one, the branch that is truly connected, and thus is totally tapped into the juice or living water of the vine, will, without exception, produce an abundance of beautiful fruit—fruit that can be considered only in the realm of what Jesus came to this earth to harvest. Jesus came to "seek and to save that which was lost" (Luke 19:10) and if we don't see the "lost" coming to Him through our lives then, quite frankly, there has to be some barrier causing a disruption of the flow of sap from the vine to the branch.

The second reality stems from the harsh cause and effect of those branches that appear to be connected to the vine yet are producing no fruit. You see these branches talk a good talk in that they were baptized, they go to church, they pay their tithes, they accept a church duty or office, they do many good things, etcetera, but one giant thing is missing, they do not bear fruit. The ugly reality is, as non-fruit-bearing plant appendages, they will soon find themselves cut off, thrown into a pile, and burned.

Thus, now that we know what the ultimate destiny is for those whose lives are not totally connected with their Savior, and we move through the critical stage of admitting that we have a problem, we are then ready to move on to discovering what step two entails—a step that will make all the difference. This step is based entirely on the small, yet powerfully significant, four-letter word, seek. Its significance is exposed through a very simple, yet monumentally powerful cause-and-effect promise found in Matthew 7:7 where it states: "Seek, and you will find." It seems nearly incomprehensible to believe that it takes only five words to lay out a solution so big, yet so simple, that the fate of literally millions, if not billions, of self-proclaimed Christians throughout the ages could have or could be totally different come judgment day. To think that there could be no cases of confusion at the gates of Heaven over who thinks they should be admitted compared to who will be admitted (referencing Matthew 7:21–23) in and of itself should make us perk up and take note. The promise is offered in such simple terms that I believe most people overlook it all together. Basically, it can be summarized as, If you want something bad enough, then get out and seek it.

The real trouble is that the solution appears so simple that we rarely ever hear it preached from the pulpits of today's Christian churches. It would seem that we would assume it be some complicated behavioral formula that requires the combined effort of lawyers and theologians to figure out and, of course, who wants that?

Alas, we would rather reduce the whole Christian experience to, "Just believe that Jesus exists and let Grace take care of the rest." As a result, we have instead focused on becoming fast-food churches to fast food-loving consumers. We have basically turned our churches into drive-through, McDonald's style eateries. We drive up to the church booth once a week to order our spiritual happy-meal: *I'll have the Trinity meal, please, the half-pound God with strips of Jesus garnished with the Holy Spirit. Let's see . . . and I'll have a Big Gulp drink of that living water stuff. Oh, and I wonder, could you super-size that for me, as you must be aware that I brought an offering today. That'll be to-go, since I'm in a bit of a hurry?*

Seeking and Finding

What does it mean to "seek"? The concept of seeking in order to find, is not simply a New Testament mandate, as we find in Matthew 7:7, but rather one that has existed since early Old Testament time. Moses, in Deuteronomy 4:29, revealed this cause-and-effect formula in the early days of the children of Israel's wanderings with these words: "But from there you will seek the Lord your God, and you will find Him if you seek Him with all your heart and with all your soul."

As a businessman, whose company offers a service to clients based on a pre-negotiated agreement, I am very much tuned to the language used in contracts. A contract's very intent is that of making sure both parties to an agreement are, first and foremost, reminded of the pre-discussed terms of their deal, as well as, secondly, that in the event that one party strays from the agreement, there is provided a means of default and thus the potential "get-out" and/or to recover damages.

For these reasons, I spend much time reviewing the fine print of the terms of a deal. As such, one of the more important parts of a contract are the "subject to's," in other words the "cause and effects" in the agreement. Examples can include: "You will be *entitled to* exercise your stock options if the company's level of sales reaches this point." Or, "You have a right *to do this* provided that takes place." And, "The validity of the entire agreement is *subject to* your paying X dollars by date Y . . ."

Along that line of contractual thought, Matthew 7:7 simply says, "You are not going to find a relationship with Jesus unless to you are willing to do something"—and that is, unless you *seek* Him.

You might conclude: *That seems simple enough. All I have to do is "seek" and I am going to be rewarded with a relationship with Jesus.* Upon reflecting on your own experience in combination with that of the simplicity of the promise, though, you may also find yourself asking, *Then why doesn't it work?* And in answer to that question, it is imperative that we first look at what does the word seek actually mean, then, second, establish what level of seeking God expects of us.

In terms of the word "seek," a dictionary definition makes one point clear: "seek" is synonymous with action. There is nothing passive about the act of seeking. If you seek, you are doing something as opposed to sitting around waiting for something to happen. That is, if you want to "find," then you had better be prepared to be busy. The problem with simply defining the word "seek" and then trying to apply it, is the fact that there are obviously different understandings as to the level of seeking that is required in order to secure a relationship with Jesus. You see most people, as dictated by time and energy constraints primarily, look to what is the minimum amount they have to invest to get what they want. *What is the minimum amount of study I need to put forth to pass the test? What is the minimum down payment in order to buy the house or car? What is the minimum number of years I need to work in order to be eligible for retirement benefits?*

Unfortunately, though, this minimalistic mentality is most often reflective of the average Christian seeking Jesus as well. To some, the level of seeking in order to find may be simply going to church once a week, and then concluding that is enough. For many of these people, seeking Jesus is reduced to nothing more than believing that they are seeking by simply spending some time around their Christian friends in church. Others may understand seeking as enrolling in a monastery to spend the rest of their life in both celibacy as well as quiet meditation. Still others find themselves engaging in deep and fervent prayer and Bible study for upwards of hours spent each day.

Herein lies one of the biggest problems found within Christianity: There appears to be no bench-mark of understanding about what God may expect in terms of how much effort we are to put into the act of seeking. It seems every churchgoer is left to merely endorse their own definition of what it means to seek and, as such, they wind up in a state of being more concerned about securing a feeling of spiritual self-contentment than they are on focusing on a dynamic relationship with Jesus.

I truly hate to put it this way but so often we treat Jesus as we would a "cheap trick," which is a rather crass way of referring to buying the services of a prostitute. We want all the benefits that come with marriage, but we don't want the commitment associated with it. To understand what I mean by this, all we need to do is look back on our past and reflect on those times when we have most passionately pursued Jesus. Isn't it during those times when trouble is either lurking at our door or has us fully in its grip? How fervent are our prayers during the times when everything seems to be going well compared to when trouble is invading our space? If our prayer life and relationship pursuit is highest during the bad times and tapers off during the good times, then just maybe Jesus has become a "hooker" to us, in that it is only when we need something from Him that we find ourselves on His doorstep. You see, no relationship will ever develop nor will it survive if there is not something serious, like time and unwavering commitment, put into it.

Therefore, it is absolutely imperative, for our very salvation, that we pursue a full understanding of what the little word "seek" actually means, that is according to God.

Bible Study

Before we begin looking at God's expectation of what it means to seek, it is of utmost importance to first identify how we are to seek. If we don't know what it means to seek, or how one is supposed to engage in the act of seeking, then it does us little good to try to understand the level to which God expects such activity. The Bible gives us two basic means of seeking.

One method of seeking can be found in 2 Timothy 2:15, where it states, "Study to shew thyself approved unto God, a workman that needeth not to be ashamed, rightly dividing the word of truth" (KJV).

This verse is suggesting that we are to "study" something in order to be "approved" for something else. Being approved for anything in life, credit cards, loans, professional associations, etcetera, is most always a rewarding experience to us personally, because it means we are accepted by the approving person or entity. So then, who better to be approved by than our Lord?

It should be of interest to us to understand that to be approved of God results in qualifying us for something great for Him—that of being a "workman that needeth not to be ashamed" of what we produce. Properly interpreted, serious study of the Bible will lead to us becoming living agents for Jesus—agents who are not ashamed of such calling to the level of exhibiting a boldness beyond our own human character.

If studying the Bible is supposed to benefit us in this way, then we must differentiate between studying the Bible itself and not books written about the Bible. As I noted earlier, one of the rigid policies I adopted before I actually found Jesus was that I was not going to read any contemporary human writings in front of or in place of Scripture. The Bible would be what I studied, nothing else. Although that was my practice for a couple of years early on and I believe it was the best thing I could have ever done, I have since taken to reading, what I consider to be, other inspired books but I maintain another rigid policy, that of I never displace my hour or more of Bible study a day with something else. You see, John 14:26 made it clear to me when it states: "But the Helper, the Holy Spirit, whom the Father will send in My name, He will teach you all things, and bring to your remembrance all things that I said to you."

For the first time in my spiritual pursuit, I understood that I was given a personal tutor whose role it was to guide me through the study of the Bible. If this were true, then I would no longer need to turn to men or women of supposed understanding in order to grasp the deep truths of the Holy Bible. My role would be to spend a serious amount of time in the Bible and thus allow the Holy Spirit actual quality time to teach me.

Just why I should want to engage in this teacher/student role can be expressed through an understanding of what the Bible can and will offer me in return for spending time studying it. In 2 Timothy 3:16 Paul offers this: "All Scripture is given by inspiration of God, and is profitable for doctrine, for reproof, for correction, for instruction in righteousness." If Scripture is to be considered profitable for all of these things, doctrine, reproof, correction and instruction, then it should be considered very logical to invest my time and effort into studying something of such potential impact.

Jesus and Prayer

The second means of seeking Jesus is through prayer. 1 Thessalonians 5:17 says, "Pray without ceasing." Certainly it should be common sense to anyone that time spent in communication with whoever it is that we wish to develop a relationship, is of critical importance. It is impossible to develop a relationship with any other person if no communication takes place. It is only through gradually exposing our innermost souls to one another that we can begin to develop the foundation on which all relationships are built, that of trust.

Because communication is a two-way activity, it behooves us to understand just how we are to engage in back and forth dialogue with a God who is both physically unseen as well as, seemingly, audibly mute. In simple response to that dilemma, prayer becomes a primary way for us to talk to God, while Bible study becomes the primary means of God talking and communicating with us. We talk to God through prayer and God talks to us through His Holy Word, the Bible. What then becomes of critical importance to understand is that of what level of prayer and Bible study are we to engage in, in order to find the relationship promised in the "seek and you shall find" promise?

In response to that question, let us first look at what God means when He says, through Paul, in 1 Thessalonians 5:17, that we are to "pray without ceasing." Since we are instructed to "walk just as He [Jesus] walked" (1 John 2:6) and to "follow His [Jesus'] steps" (1 Peter 2:21), then it is critical that we look to Jesus to see how much time He invested in prayer with His Father. Before we look at Jesus as our example though, I think it is important to make clear the fact that Jesus was and is the Son of God, albeit while on this earth He took on the full cloak of humanity. As the Son of God and as a Man who lived a life completely devoid of sin, it could be concluded that Jesus would have needed less prayer time than we sin-sick, feeble human beings. As a result of such conclusion, it needs to be plainly stated that it would only make sense for us take the kind of time Jesus spent in prayer and then multiply it by a whole bunch to arrive at the level of time we should be spending in order to arrive at Paul's suggested level of "pray[ing] without ceasing."

Thus, looking to Jesus' example, we read in Mark 1:35, that "in the morning, having risen a long while before daylight, He went out and departed to a solitary place; and there He prayed." What priority was Jesus manifesting, so early in the morning that it was still dark? He quietly got up, slipped away to a place of solitude and there prayed. Looking at the demanding life Jesus lived with throngs of needy people constantly pressing in on Him, we would have to conclude that if anyone needed to sleep in a bit, in an attempt to garner a little more energy for the day, it was Him. Instead, we find Him in the quiet and stillness of the early morning, pouring out His heart to the sole source of His strength, that of His Father.

Looking further to Jesus as our example, Matthew 14:23 reads: "And when He had sent the multitudes away, He went up on the mountain by Himself to pray. Now when evening came, He was alone there." Here we again find Jesus, alone, praying. To catch a glimpse of this "sacrifice" of energy and time, we need only look at how exhausting his days would have been. To be traveling around on foot, no buses, cars, or horse-drawn carriages, at a minimum, would have been physically exhausting. But then add to that the constant draw on His energy source of needy people wanting to be close to Him would have been hugely taxing as well. With people crowding in on Him, all wanting to be heard and wanting their spiritual as well as physical needs met, plus to have the religious leaders constantly badgering Him with trick questions and insults, to say nothing of not even having time to quietly eat, would have left Him sucked dry and in desperate need of quiet time and sleep. But, still, Jesus found it necessary to slip away from the hustle and bustle of His day so that He could then spend time in prayer with His Father.

And if that doesn't loudly proclaim the need of prayer by God's dear Son, we need only look at Luke 6:12: "Now it came to pass in those days that He went out to the mountain to pray, and continued all night in prayer to God." When was the last time you felt it necessary to spend an entire night in deep communion with God through prayer because you felt empty and devoid of a connection with the King of kings and Lord of lords?

When we are admonished to "pray without ceasing," we are not then left without an example. One would think that if anyone could get away with less time in prayer than you and me, it should have been Jesus. Even though He had taken on full humanity, certainly He would have understood the uniqueness of His mission here and, from that fact, could have rested on His divine connection. Instead, He understood it vital to continually stay connected in prayer with His Father in Heaven. Thus, He prayed often and long.

In view of our seeking a meaningful relationship with Jesus, how, then, can we, as sinful human beings, ever think that we can somehow get away with less time spent in prayer than did Jesus?

Seeking First

Next, though, we need to pursue and understand what the "seek" in the seek-and-you-shall-find formula actually looks like in terms of biblical intent. As we discovered, the Bible clearly lays out two primary means of engaging ourselves in the act of seeking—that is, studying and praying. We now need to attempt to better understand the second step in our process, which is the actual level of seeking expected in order to secure the dynamic relationship with Jesus. It is the step that will lead us to the path of abundant living as talked of in John 10:10—"I have come that they may have life, and that they may have it more abundantly."

In order to begin understanding the level of seeking suggested in the Bible, though, we need to first and foremost look at one of the most encompassing promises in the New Testament, that of Matthew 6:31–33. It states: "Therefore do not worry, saying, 'What shall we eat?' or 'What shall we drink?' or 'What shall we wear?' For after all these things the Gentiles seek. For your heavenly Father knows that you need all these things. But seek first the kingdom of God and His righteousness, and all these things shall be added to you."

This text clearly challenges us to look at our priorities in life in order to determine where the pursuit of Jesus sits in relation to *everything else*. The sticky part comes when we must consider which is more important: working hard to cover our basic needs or ignoring them and instead pursuing a God we can't even see? After all, who doesn't have a concern for the very basic necessities of life? Of course, God wants us to have them, but He is saying here is, "Leave those worries and pursuits up to me. I am fully capable of providing for your needs. All I want you to do is put Me ahead of everything else in your life. I want you to make Me your number one priority so that I can show you what an 'abundant life' actually looks like."

The mere fact that we are told to seek Jesus first, above everything else, connotes an act that is probably outside the realm of most human comprehension. First and foremost, we are supposed to pursue with passion a God that we physically cannot see. Yes, we can see signs that He is there just as we can see signs that wind exists, but we have not been given the ability or access to gaze upon Him in His physical form. We are simply left record that He both exists as well as deeply loves and cares for us personally.

Now, armed with a basic belief that He does exist, we are to forget about what we think is humanly important and, instead, pursue a relationship with Him. The tough part of this whole plan is that it appears, on the surface anyhow, to make no sense.

I cannot personally fathom how God is literally going to put food on my table if my attention is not on directly procuring such staple. How is He going to make sure my kids have clothes, and that their education is going to be paid for? What about my rent or mortgage? If I don't make those items a priority, my family will more than likely end up on the street with all our earthly possessions stacked around our feet.

The strange part is that God rarely engages us to do what makes sense, but rather, He always seems to force us to leave common sense behind and to venture into the realm of the seemingly senseless. In other words, it seems that either God has a way of complicating my pursuit of a relationship with Him, or my comprehension of the way He operates is tainted with human interpretation. Why not just be there with us, rather than making us shift everything around in our lives so that we can somehow find Him at the end of some road of pursuit? No, instead God, a self-proclaimed jealous God (Exodus 20:5 says, "for I the Lord your God am a jealous God") has chosen to make us pursue Him with undivided attention in order to have the relationship with Him that ultimately ends in our living a superior and abundant life.

Unfortunately though, as we have been learning so far, it is not always as easy and as simple as it seems at first glance. Yes, all we have to do is seek in order to find Jesus, but then we encounter a text like Matthew 6:31–33 which puts a qualifier on the statement. In other words (Jesus speaking), "It isn't just 'seek' that I want from you, but rather, a seeking to the level of me becoming more important in your life than absolutely everything and anything else that exists."

With All Our Heart

To build on the process of attempting to understand just what level of seeking God expects us to put into the pursuit of His "only begotten Son" of John 3:16, we will have a look at the cause and effect of Deuteronomy 4:29. In it we find boldly stated: "But from there you will seek the Lord your God, and you will find Him if you seek Him with all your heart and with all your soul."

First and foremost, whenever and wherever we see the little-big word *if*, we should always stop right there and ask ourselves the question, "What is the term of condition upon which this promise is to be met?" The word "if," in and of itself, connotes a condition or "subject to," upon which this promise can and will be delivered. In essence it is saying, "Don't expect anything to happen until such time as you engage in the 'cause' to the level specified."

Through this text, we begin to get a better understanding of what it means to "seek ye first" by way of looking at the qualifier upon which the "thou shalt find" is to be met. How much effort will those who have found Jesus have put into seeking their Lord? They will have sought Jesus with "all their heart and with all their soul." According to this reference, there is certainly expected a level of seeking that goes far beyond mere church attendance. As a further qualifier, Hebrews 11:6 adds to the point by stating that the one who comes "to God must believe that He is, and that He is a rewarder of those who diligently seek Him."

According to Paul, there is no such thing as being rewarded a dynamic relationship with Jesus with any effort short of a diligent pursuit of Jesus. To engage in the pursuit of one's personal Savior in a passive manner, one of convenience whereby we try to fit Jesus in here or there, will not produce results. An all or nothing level of pursuit is required, at a minimum, to produce even the most miniscule amount of relationship development.

Jesus, after all, left us an example of what that undivided pursuit will, not may, look like. In Matthew 6:24, He states: "No one can serve two masters; for either he will hate the one and love the other, or else he will be loyal to the one and despise the other. You cannot serve God and mammon." There is to be no two-timing with another lover if we are going to consider Jesus to be the single love of our lives. Paul also chose to make this point clear when, in 1 Corinthians 10:21 and 22 he wrote: "You cannot drink the cup of the Lord and the cup of demons; you cannot partake of the Lord's table and of the table of demons. Or do we provoke the Lord to jealousy? Are we stronger than He?" Clearly, there is to be no spiritually adulterous affair with the devil if Jesus is to be considered our marriage mate. In fact, he gets right in our face with a couple of insinuating questions, that of, *Do we provoke the Lord to jealousy? Are we stronger than is He?* In regard to the idea of whether or not we can get away with keeping one foot tap-dancing in the world while the other is walking the road to Heaven, God lets us in on a point that should wake us up to the reality of the level of allegiance that He expects in order to have and maintain a solid relationship with Him.

In Exodus 20:5, in the heart of the Ten Commandments, we read: "I, the Lord your God, am a jealous God." Obviously Paul was aware of this Old Testament scriptural reference, which is why he chose to make his bold point by way of asking the modernized question: "Are we going to provoke Jesus by dancing with another partner to the level of making Him jealous?" Of course, God doesn't suffer from the same type of cheap jealousy humans often have. Rather, God's jealously is deeply rooted in love. God loves us for our benefit and He does not want us to lose out on the benefits of a relationship with Him, the Gift-giver. He makes it ever so clear as to where He is coming from in the love relationship He so wants with us.

In Jeremiah 29:11 we read that God wants us to fully understand His position in the potential relationship with us: "For I know the thoughts that I think toward you, says the Lord, thoughts of peace and not of evil, to give you a future and a hope." God is the single source of love in the universe, and as such, we would have to actually deviate from the biblical record itself to endorse a belief that God can harbor both evil as well as good thoughts towards us. Jesus so wanted to expose the fact that what you see in Him is what you get with God, that He outright informed us of it. In John 14:9 He says that "He who has seen Me has seen the Father." And, then, if that isn't enough, He uses a parallel in Matthew 7:9–11 to explain it further, asking, "What man is there among you who, if his son asks for bread, will give him a stone? Or if he asks for a fish, will he give him a serpent? If you then, being evil, know how to give good gifts to your children, how much more will your Father who is in heaven give good things to those who ask Him!"

How can a relationship of any kind survive if the giving is all one-sided? If we choose to believe that God is there to give us good things, but without any serious commitment or input to the relationship on our part, then we are sadly mistaken to the level of ultimately being rejected at heaven's very gates.

The "seek" part of a relationship development with Jesus is not to be underestimated. Adding to the Bible's interpretation of what level of input is expected from us in order for us to "find" is Jeremiah's quotation of God Himself, in Jeremiah 29:13: "And you will seek Me and find Me, when you search for Me with all your heart." Based on this, I believe it important to at least ponder the question, *What would the pursuit of Jesus look like if we were to put out entire heart into the process?*

Of Love, Courtship, and Marriage

I guess one way we could answer this question is to convert it into human relationship terms and ask: *How much time would I consider is just enough in order to adequately court a potential spouse for marriage?* Is it even in the realm of sanity to look at courtship and marriage in terms of what is the minimum I can get away with in order to get to the altar and then proceed in a marriage relationship?

Married men, I don't know about you, but I couldn't see enough of my girlfriend for the two years we dated before we married. I never once pondered the thought of, *I wonder if I could get away with seeking less—of spending less time with the love of my life and still get to the altar.* No, mine, as well as hers, was literally a passionate pursuit of the other with laughing, joking, teasing and perpetual flirting providing the content of rich and joyous times together.

"Just how much is enough in order to get by in a love-relationship?" is, in and of itself, a flawed question in that it connotes a complete lack of priority. To target the minimum required in our pursuit of a relationship with Jesus boldly declares that Jesus is definitely not our number one priority but rather a luxury to be had whenever we need Him. Most Christians truly like, if not love, the thought of having Jesus around but when He becomes an accessory, a back-up plan or a go-to-God when in trouble, we have reduced Him to the level of a the prostitute talked of above, whereby we say, in essence, "I want all the benefits that come with marriage, but I don't want the commitment."

When "love is in the air", time spent together is never measured in terms of minimums but rather enters the realm of how can I spend more time with the one I want to have a relationship with?

Learning and Knowledge

Clearly, according to Scripture, there is no such thing as expecting big returns from little investment or input. Thus, we have to make our quest, our seeking of Jesus, the most important activity in our life. Even a genius like Albert Einstein himself understood the futility of not stepping out of the status quo in order to expect new things to happen. He actually added to the definition of "insanity" suggesting it is to carry on with life as usual yet expect something big and new to turn up on your doorstep. His definition should, at a minimum, jolt the Laodicean Christians who figure they are on the path of relationship development with Jesus but instead are living in a stupor. When "going through the motions" is the best that could be said of the level of their pursuit of Jesus, then "to hell" is probably the most apt description of their direction of travel.

According to Scripture, there is no such thing as a shortcut to the development of a real and meaningful relationship with Jesus.

One of my favorite explanations of the level of seeking that God demands of those who actually desire a passionate relationship with Jesus is Proverbs 2:3–5. This cause and effect promise delivers a plain and simple analogous example of the level of seeking expected of us: "Yes, if you cry out for discernment, and lift up your voice for understanding, if you seek her as silver, and search for her as for hidden treasures; then you will understand the fear of the Lord, and find the knowledge of God."

When it talks of pursuing "knowledge" and "understanding," it is talking of much more than the cerebral learning of Scripture. Paul, writing to Timothy, differentiated "learning" from that of "knowledge." When talking of the sinful and callused state of the carnal "Christian" man, he stated that there were two identifying characteristics surrounding their type.

First, they "had a form of godliness, but denied its power" (2 Timothy 3:5) and, second, they were "always learning, and never able to come to the knowledge of truth" (2 Timothy 3:7).

It must be understood that there is a marked difference between learning and knowledge. Learning is the cerebral gathering of facts and details about the Bible and its characters, while knowledge is based on the root word, to *know,* meaning to "have a relationship with." Over many years of speaking at institutions of higher learning, I have delivered more than once warned students: "Beware, you could very easily spend four to six years of your life studying in this institution and come out with a ton of learning under your belt but be devoid of knowledge."

Thus, when Solomon, in Proverbs 2, talks of pursuing "knowledge" and "understanding," he is referring to something more than simply learning facts from the Bible. He is instead referring to developing a relationship with our Creator. What is most critical to understand in this passage, though, is how much effort we are to put into finding a relationship with Jesus. To get his point across with more urgency, he uses the analogy of the effort a prospector puts into searching for precious metal or hidden treasures as a comparison of the level of effort expected of us in our pursuit of Jesus.

An Analogy

This passage is of such vivid impact to me because I grew up in the bush of northern British Columbia, Canada, where prospectors and trappers plied their trade. Many of these prospectors could be observed panning and sluicing for gold within eyesight of where we lived on the banks of the Fraser River. Because the river was the highway on which boat travel displaced that of trudging through bush, devoid of roads, we many times had an unexpected visitor of the prospector type, who would nose his long, planked river boat onto the shore below our houses and wander up the bank for a visit and maybe a welcomed hot drink or meal of moose-meat stew. During these occasional visits, I was treated to the most titillating experience any kid, devoid of television and the intrusion of media, could ever hope to gain access. To add my wild imagination to hearing real-life stories of run-ins with wild animals, of escapes from overturned boats, of gold found and then stolen or lost, was above and beyond anything the most dramatic movie could ever portray.

Being influenced by the direct stories of these men, I, later on, made it a habit of carrying a gold pan, a small pick and a military fold-up shovel, all tucked into a knapsack in the back of my jeep. As I had spent years of my spare time doing what I loved best, that of exploring the British Columbia wilderness, I would occasionally come across a beautiful little creek. Since there was always that chance of winning the lottery by finding a rich vein of gold, I would stop, take out my pan and shovel and sluice a few quick pans. The good news was that I nearly always was rewarded with finding "color," meaning I would find a few flakes of gold amid the sand in the bottom of my pan.

Reflecting on it today, though, I would have to say that I was never anything more than a casual prospector, as I would simply delight in finding the color and that would suffice. The difference between the real prospectors I met and me was that while finding a bit of color was always good enough for me, a bit of color to them was the fuel on which their passion burned—gold fever.

So to bring Solomon's analogy to its intended point: It is basically a matter of gold fever versus "God fever." We have the freedom to be one or the other. We can be a passive church-going Laodicean or a passionate pursuer of Jesus. The weekender prospector will be content with a little bit of Jesus-color in their life, while the passionate pursuer of Jesus perceives the color only as an indicator of the mother-lode to be discovered and mined. The passive pursuer of Jesus will never experience the full, rich blessing found by those who passionately pursue Jesus.

Another Analogy

Imagine that I am an old man failing in health who, through many years of world travel and adventure had made a shocking discovery. No one knows for sure just what part of the world I made this discovery in, but what they all do know is that I happened upon a magnificent hidden treasure of gold, jewels and priceless artifacts. To validate my discovery, I had selected a few pieces from the cache of treasure and showed them to the world's leading historians and analysts. All agreed that I had definitely discovered the lost treasure of the ancient nation of Tilmour. The gold coins from which I selected samples were clearly from that nation, and the couple of the gems I had chosen were documented as being part of the Queen of Tilmour's vast collection of priceless jewels. Historic records also had it that the pirating of the ship carrying such treasure was the most expensive loss in the history of thievery and high sea transport.

For all practical reasons, I had, through my life, developed a full understanding of the curse associated with newfound wealth (as can be observed today through the lives of those who self-destruct upon winning multi-million dollar lotteries), so I had simply chosen not to go back and claim the treasure. Unfortunately, and as could be expected, my life, from the point of discovery on to the present, has been fraught with intrusions of the magnitude of having my phone bugged, my every move placed under surveillance, people attempting to blackmail me, as well as attempted court orders to get me to divulge the treasure's whereabouts.

To add further proof to the validity of my find is the fact that everyone knows only too well that I am also considered by everyone in society to be the most credible and honest man anyone has ever met. My word is pure gold, my intentions purely honest and upright and as a result there has never been one question by anyone as to the authenticity of my claim of discovery. No one has ever questioned even a fragment of my description of how massive and magnificent the hidden treasure truly is simply because of both my credibility as an honest and upright person as well as the proof I have given to society through the actual pieces of treasure I provided.

It has been years of newspaper, magazine and television headlines all querying and speculating as to why I would be so crazy as not to claim the treasure I had found and then enjoy the wealth and notoriety associated with having cashed in on a find worth nearly one billion dollars in estimated value.

Such has been the case—until now.

Age finally begins to overcome me and rather quickly I find myself in an acute care hospital bed living out my labored last few hours. The halls of the hospital are jammed with hungry news reporters, all speculating about why I would go to my grave with the secret. Many are speculating that maybe I have left a secret note divulging the treasure's whereabouts. *Could there be a safety deposit box somewhere? A riddle left to lead to the treasure's location? Has a charity or a museum been willed a note of its secret place?*

Now you, like the entire rest of the world, have been breathlessly watching the news as reporters, psycho-analysts and appraisers all talk of the treasure's value, as well as the mind-defying reason that I would allow knowledge of the location to go to my grave.

Suddenly, the phone rings and you hear a soft and failing voice on the other end of the line. "Who is this?" you repeat several times.

And then you listen to the request to rush to my bedside. When the brief phone call ends, you are angry about getting this prank call. But then, there was something eerily familiar about the voice, even though laboring and faint. *Could it be? Nah, you're not so stupid as to fall for one so obvious.*

You think about it for a moment and then that little something inside you prompts you to conclude that the pride-related risk factor of responding to a prank call is extremely small in comparison to the what-if possibility. Within half an hour you are getting out of your car in the hospital parking lot. As you walk to the entrance, you are immediately accosted by one of the dozens of police patrolling the hospital's entry.

"What is the purpose of your visit here today?" one demands.

"I am not quite sure other than I got a phone call from someone claiming to be the treasure hunter, and he requested that I quickly come down to the hospital to see him."

A shocked look develops on the face of the officer as he quickly whirls around and yells to the other officers, "We have our person; let them through."

Your mind is swirling with bewilderment as you are given a personal escort through the throng of clamoring reporters. Within a few moments you are standing by my bedside and, before I speak to you, I say to everyone else, "Can we have a moment to ourselves, please?"

As the room empties of its occupants, your heart begins to pound as all sorts of thoughts race through you: *What if . . . Could it be? What am I going to say in response?*

And then I turn to you and, in a near inaudible voice, speak: "Young man/woman, as you more than likely know, I had made a discovery a number of years ago, a discovery that I didn't want to capitalize on since I really didn't want the attention nor the hassles associated with having to manage such a great wealth. But I have done a lot of thinking lately, and I have decided that I am willing to share my secret with someone who I believe could both handle the great responsibility of the money as well as, more importantly, would know how to use the money to make a difference in other people's lives. I have searched long and hard, trying to find a person who I believe could fulfill that roll. I don't have time to tell you how I found your name but what I do want to tell you is that your kindness and unmatched love for others less fortunate than yourself is what I was looking for in a candidate for sharing my secret. I would now like you to take that pen right there and write down a number, a number that will lead you to a small, uninhabited, unnamed island in the South Pacific. It is there that you will find the hidden treasure. You have my word on it."

You shakily reach out and take the pen and the small piece of paper lying on the nightstand beside my bed and you lean in close so you can clearly hear what I have to say.

In a weak and faltering voice you listen intently as I state: "The GPS reading that will lead you right to the island on which the treasure will be found is . . ." And with that, I dictate to you a well-memorized number, a number that will put you within a one-square-mile range of the very source of the world's greatest treasure.

Your heart is pounding as you fold up the paper and place it in your front pocket where it will be safe from intruding eyes. As you look up to prepare to pour out your heartfelt thanks, you watch in heart-breaking horror as I heave one last deep breath and die.

Now, how about a few questions?

What does this story do to you? The questions that we must all answer right here are that of, *What will your life be like now? Will it be more of the same old routine? Will it be like: Well, that was interesting but I really need to hurry along right now because I have to pick up the kids to take them to soccer?*

In other words, if you do choose to pursue the promised treasure, will your prospecting efforts be that of a couple of hours of passive seeking and searching each weekend in church, maybe a vain repetition before each meal you eat or a quick and meaningless prayer before you turn out the light at night? Could you possibly be satisfied anymore with the nine-to-five, mind-numbing routine of your everyday work schedule when you know that there lies hidden, on a one square mile island deep in the South Pacific, a treasure worth hundreds of millions of dollars?

Solomon used this analogy to expose the kind of pursuit that burns within the true prospector or treasure hunter in order to get us to understand the level of passionate desire that must permeate our search for Jesus. There is no shortcut to developing a relationship with Christ. It must be understood that there is flawless credibility behind all of God's promises. When He says, "Seek and you will find" you can be rest assured that you are going to find a treasure at the end of the search; if, that is, you search with the passion as described in the Bible.

CHAPTER 10

NO VACANCY

As the illustration in the last chapter showed, God's word is "gold." We have no reason to doubt a single thing He has promised. And then, in addition to being impeccably credible, He has gone so far as to actually show us evidence of the treasure He promises. With open hand, God reached out and displayed the most magnificent treasure to ever be observed. He left us the following record as proof of His intent. "For God so loved the world that He gave His only begotten Son, that whoever believes in Him should not perish but have everlasting life" (John 3:16).

There can be no mistake: When God says, "You will find the treasure I offer you," He means exactly that. The supreme agony Jesus endured at Satan's murderous hands was not so much the physical pain and suffering but rather the cold separation from His Father as a result of bearing our sin, all to put a value on the sacrificial offering. The sin bearer was only a small sample of the level of love to be found in the treasure of the ages, a treasure we are guaranteed, by blood, if we would only seek to the level of Biblical expectation.

God does not only boldly declare the level of His expectation when He says "seek" in the breadth of His meaning ("diligently seek Him"; "search for me will all your heart"; "if you seek Him with all your heart and with all your soul"; "seek as you would silver and hid treasure" etcetera), but He also gives us many more subtle hints as well, of which hints are meant to direct us to the understanding that Jesus isn't to be considered available like one would order a meal at the drive through window at McDonalds. In other words, "come Lord Jesus quickly because I have a hunger pang right this minute" and yet when things are going well in life, we could really care less whether or not He is an every-moment-type friend.

As just one example of a more subtle, yet powerful suggestion of the level of pursuit expected in our "seeking", we can find a somewhat obscure, yet powerful revelation found in Matthew 12:43–45. I must admit that this reference had always disturbed me more than a little in that it seems we can be left without a defense system against the powers of darkness. Its rather chilly-feeling message is as follows: "When an unclean spirit goes out of a man, he goes through dry places, seeking rest, and finds none. Then he says, 'I will return to my house from which I came.' And when he comes, he finds it empty, swept, and put in order. Then he goes and takes with him seven other spirits more wicked than himself, and they enter and dwell there; and the last state of that man is worse than the first. So shall it also be with this wicked generation."

The Sign of Jonah

To think that, first of all, a demon could ever find justification to inhabit a so-called Christian was hard enough; but then to think that once cast out, it would have the freedom and liberty to reenter is even a more challenging thought. And then to make matters worse, it appears that the solo demon could easily bring along a few friends, seven to be exact, and create more of a problem than before.

How could this be possible? To gain an understanding of this rather disturbing text, I began by reading and rereading the passage as well as its preface in an attempt to understand its context, and finally, after seeming to get nowhere in interpretation, I prayed my familiar prayer: "Holy Spirit, Jesus promised that you will be my teacher and my guide and as such I am informing you that I will not leave this spot today until you have given me the key to understanding what this passage is all about." For the next two hours I pleaded for an answer and then, suddenly, it hit me.

The stage is set by backing up to verse 38 of Matthew 12. There we observe the Pharisees challenging Jesus to prove Himself. "Then some of the scribes and Pharisees answered, saying, 'Teacher, we want to see a sign from You.'" Obviously, they wanted their own proof-party, so that they could figure what was behind Jesus' power and draw. Jesus' response was something we should take to heart today, especially when we find ourselves demanding He prove Himself to us through a healing or some other obvious or sensational miracle.

Verse 39 relays Jesus' answer to the Pharisees' demand: "He answered and said to them, an evil and adulterous generation seeks after a sign, and no sign will be given to it except the sign of the prophet Jonah."

It may seem puzzling to us today, after reviewing all the open miracles Jesus performed within the four gospels, to try to figure out why Jesus simply didn't go one step further and give them what they were asking for. It could have provided enough proof to at least some of the religious elite to lead them to understand that only God could make this kind of thing happen, and—even though they probably would not have openly admitted it among their peers—some good may have taken place. Instead, in essence, He boldly states that because you are so far off-base in your religious beliefs, I am not going to give you any sign except, that is, "the sign of the prophet Jonas."

I think it logical to immediately let curiosity loose and wonder, What is that all about? What is the sign of Jonah? One has to look no further than the very next statement (verse 40) to begin to get an understanding of what Jesus was referring to here. It states: "For as Jonah was three days and three nights in the belly of the great fish, so will the Son of Man be three days and three nights in the heart of the earth." First of all, we should get more than a hint that Jesus is attempting to convey a parallel of His own story and ministry with that of Jonah's. In other words, if we look at what Jonah was commissioned to deliver to the Ninevites, we should be able to find a parallel as to what Jesus came to accomplish as well.

Dropping back to the Old Testament record of Jonah's story, we find what God's mission for Jonah was. Jonah 1:2 and verse 3:2 respectively state the mission God engaged him to accomplish. God said: "Arise, go to Nineveh, that great city, and cry out against it; for their wickedness has come up before Me . . . and preach to it the message that I tell you."

By observing the record of what Jonah preached, in response to God's commission, we recognize that he was to preach a warning message: "Repent from your wicked ways or else destruction will befall you in forty days." Events recorded in the book of Jonah reveal that the Ninevites did wake up to the warning and repented, thus allowing God to again place His hand of protection over them.

Very clearly, Jesus was putting together a comparison and contrast between His own mission on planet earth with that of what Jonah was sent to reveal to a wayward people. Three days and three nights in a whale's belly verses three days and three nights, to come, in the heart of the earth could not be a more direct hint. It was meant both as a warning to the self-righteous religious who were walking a wayward path as well as expose the seriousness of the consequence if the warning were not heeded. If repentance were neglected, eternal death would most certainly follow.

Now, going back to verse 41 of Matthew 12 we observe another parallel: the Ninevites themselves are used as a contrast to the Sadducees and Pharisees and their response to Jesus' warning message. "The men of Nineveh will rise up in the judgment with this generation and condemn it, because they repented at the preaching of Jonah; and indeed a greater than Jonah is here."

What Jesus is not so subtly divulging is that the pompous so-called religious leaders of His day will be judged. The element that differentiated the two, that of the Old Testament Ninevites with that of the Pharisaical bunch whom Jesus was attempting to warn, was the fact that the Ninevites actually gave credence to their warning and repented, meaning they did an about face from their old sinful ways and chose God. Jesus then goes on to say that this act of repentance qualified the Ninevites to judge those who chose to reject the contemporary warning they were receiving and to remain resolute in their evil.

Now that Jesus delivered His seemingly, politically incorrect assessment of the religious zealots, He brings Himself into the comparison

He first introduced in verse 40, that of Jonah and Himself. Jesus wants the Pharisees to understand that although Jonah was mighty in the evangelistic commission he carried out, there was One present who was more qualified and powerful in the delivery of a warning than God's messenger of old. Of course Jesus presented that part of the warning as more than a subtle hint, which the self-righteous recipients could take or leave.

The Queen of the South Jesus now moves on to another comparison, which He meant to be a point of monumental importance to the self-proclaimed religious elite. In verse 42 He states, "The queen of the South will rise up in the judgment with this generation and condemn it, for she came from the ends of the earth to hear the wisdom of Solomon; and indeed a greater than Solomon is here."

Here Jesus again uses another well-known Old Testament story to drive home a point meant to make the Pharisees and Sadducees aware of what they were missing in their spiritual pursuits. In other words, were they really seeking God, as we have all been told to do, or were they just playing the religion game, that of seeking to protect only their own positions in church? It's a question we all need to ask ourselves as well.

Moving on, Jesus says the queen of the south, obviously referring to the Queen of Sheba (as found in the book of 1 Kings 10), had also engaged in something considered of such noble righteousness as to warrant her also rising up in judgment against the Pharisaical religious and their followers. What did she do to be considered of such righteousness to judge others? Since only one fact is given here, it must be of great spiritual relevance. The reference says that "she came from the ends of the earth to hear the wisdom of Solomon."

In other words, the queen dropped everything of apparent importance in her life as her nation's leader, temporarily gave up her life of convenience and luxury and then greatly sacrificed her comfort by enduring all the struggles associated with travel in those days, all in attempt to garner insight into the success of the great and renowned King Solomon.

And now we hear Jesus commending her for her passionate pursuit of truth and knowledge, a fact meant to create a stark contrast to the religionists Jesus was dealing with. Upon extolling the virtue He wished the Pharisees and Sadducees to grasp and understand, Jesus then again brings himself back into the comparison by stating: "indeed a greater than Solomon is here." The hint Jesus was attempting to get across was that of, when one looks at the amount of passion put into the pursuit of Solomon and then consider the fact that there is Someone standing before you who actually has the power to afford you eternal life itself, would you not think that there should be a greater amount of passion expended in the pursuit of this person? The obvious point being, "no passive, lack-luster pursuit of me, the Son of God, is ever going to result in a personal relationship between the two of us. It will only happen if you choose to seek Him first, above all other pursuits to show that your heart is not going to be shared with mammon (Matthew 6:24) or, in other words, shared with alternate loves.

The Demons

Now that we have dissected the lead-up to Matthew 12:43-45 where the removed demon freely coming back, along with seven other demons, we can observe how it things fit together.

First, there had to be some event or happening that drove the demon out in the first place. That event is clearly conveyed through "the sign of the prophet Jonah." Jonah issued a warning complete with a proposed solution: Repent of your sinful ways. The Ninevites, in turn, were willing to wake up to the reality that they had a problem (the first step in finding Jesus) and as such needed a solution, the solution obviously being to repent and then give control of their lives over to God. Their very act of repentance in turn destroyed the demons' rightful claim to inhabit, and thus it was given an eviction notice, that of, "Get out now!" Of course the solo demon was forced to evacuate its host (verse 43), which leads it to seeking another person to inhabit. ("When an unclean spirit goes out of a man, he goes through dry places, seeking rest, and finds none.")

An interesting action then occurs. Since the demon is not able to find a new host and is not content to remain homeless, it decides to go back and check out its old habitat. Upon arrival, it is somewhat shocked and surprised to see that its former home is not only empty, but looking rather neat, clean and very inviting. Specifically, in verse 44, it says, "Then he says, 'I will return to my house from which I came.' And when he comes, he finds it empty, swept, and put in order."

I believe the poignant question must be asked: What did the demon really expect to find when it came back? The obvious answer by any discerning Christian should be that the demon should have no doubt expected to find the host inhabited by its nemesis, Jesus. After all, it was repentance to this Jesus that caused the demon to be evicted in the first place.

The question that should then follow is: Why wasn't the host still inhabited by Jesus? It would seem that everything should have been just grand with the former host living the "abundant life" as promised in John 10:10. That person obviously responded to the warning and answered the call through repentance and probably baptism, and would have thought been impermeable to the demon's advances.

What then happened that had allowed the demon to reenter? What lesson are we supposed to learn from this story in our own quest to have an ongoing relationship with Jesus?

Bringing it Together

We must answer the question by both reviewing the events that took place in the host person in combination with the two analogies of Jonah and the Queen of Sheba. First, the host obviously had to have rejected Satan's demonic angel by choosing a new master, that of Jesus. How did the person reject Satan? It was through the commitment that the Ninevites made, that of repenting of their evil ways and making a choice to engage in a serious about-face.

The Ninevites obviously recognized that they had a spiritual problem (again first step in finding Jesus) and that there truly were two roads to travel as found in Matthew 7:13, 14: "Enter by the narrow gate; for wide is the gate and broad is the way that leads to destruction, and there are many who go in by it. Because narrow is the gate and difficult is the way which leads to life, and there are few who find it."

It became clear to them, through Jonah's preaching, that they were traveling on a popular road ultimately terminating in hell. The reason Jesus featured this truth to persuade us that serious repentance is needed to the level of radically changing our direction of travel in life.

The host person had obviously followed the same decisional path as the Ninevites, and through repentance to God was freed of possession by the demon, but something had happened during the in between time as the inhabitant was clearly missing, as the demon returns to find a "vacant" sign hanging around the neck of the host person. How could this happen as the host had obviously chosen to follow Jesus at some point?

What happened has everything to do with what Jesus is trying so desperately to get us to understand through His myriad of hints as well as bold statements of fact. The demon finds the host empty, albeit swept and clean (in other words in slightly better spiritual condition than before) but, nevertheless, Jesus isn't living there. And this is where the story of the Queen of Sheba comes in.

Through the analogy of the queen, Jesus reveals that a second action needs to take place in order to have Him perpetually occupy our lives. The key lies in not just what the queen did, but how she did it. She passionately pursued Solomon, not in a sexual way but rather in order to understand why Solomon was so incredibly blessed. She chose to abandon all responsibility and pursuits back home and in turn put together a huge and lavish assortment of gifts: "Now when the queen of Sheba heard of the fame of Solomon concerning the name of the Lord, she came to test him with hard questions. She came to Jerusalem with a very great retinue, with camels that bore spices, very much gold, and precious stones; and when she came to Solomon, she spoke with him about all that was in her heart. So Solomon answered all her questions; there was nothing so difficult for the king that he could not explain it to her. And when the queen of Sheba had seen all the wisdom of Solomon, the house that he had built, the food on his table, the seating of his servants, the service of his waiters and their apparel, his cupbearers, and his entryway by which he went up to the house of the Lord, there was no more spirit in her.

"Then she said to the king: 'It was a true report which I heard in my own land about your words and your wisdom. However I did not believe the words until I came and saw with my own eyes; and indeed the half was not told me. Your wisdom and prosperity exceed the fame of which I heard. Happy are your men and happy are these your servants, who stand continually before you and hear your wisdom! Blessed be the Lord your God, who delighted in you, setting you on the throne of Israel! Because the Lord has loved Israel forever, therefore He made you king, to do justice and righteousness.' Then she gave the king one hundred and twenty talents of gold, spices in great quantity, and precious stones. There never again came such abundance of spices as the queen of Sheba gave to King Solomon" (1 Kings 10:1–10).

The whole analogy boils down to this: the person from whom the demon had left, because of the act of repentance, had failed to enter into the all important second aspect of relationship development, that of not just seeking, but seeking with absolute passionate, number one priority. The Queen of Sheba did exactly this and then in addition, gave of her best in order to have that for which she was hungry.

The demon was probably as surprised as anyone to find the host-person empty, because if everything went as it should have in the life of a true Jesus-follower, there would have been a bold sign hanging outside declaring: "No Vacancy, Jesus Lives Here." Through this story, we are given an understanding that it may be one thing to repent and begin the process of finding a relationship with Jesus, but it is entirely another to maintain and grow that relationship through ongoing, perpetual and passionate pursuit of truth through non-other than prayer and Bible study.

Thus, a key in having the abundant life promised us, the life I had so desperately wanted, is found in that willingness to give all and surrender all to Jesus. It's one thing to seek Jesus, and even to find Him. That's crucial. But, then, once there, we need to constantly, day by day, do what the Queen of Sheba did: that of exercising the decision to totally commit to following Jesus, no matter where the path may leads.

CHAPTER 11

THE HOUR

T HUS, IN LIGHT OF THE OVERWHELMING AMOUNT OF BIBLI-
cal input given as to just what it takes to have and maintain
a relationship with Jesus, it is vitally important to now look
at what a "passionate pursuit" of truth may look like in today's rat
race, when we are so busy just doing the bare necessities. In other
words, how much time is enough time spent on the pursuit of Jesus
in order to possess a dividend-paying relationship with Him; that
is, after we know we have a problem, how can we work on fixing it?

Time Use

Since passion requires the input of both time and energy, it behooves us to, at a minimum, take a serious look at the pie diagram
of time allotment in life in order to attempt to discover where and
how much of that diagram will be labeled, "Time spent one-on-one
with Jesus." According to the Bible, and its interpretation of what it
means to seek, Jesus is not to be offered our crumbs of time or the

leftovers after everything else in life is dealt with. So just what would our time-pie look like once it has been fully cut up and dispersed?

First of all, we all seem to know about the time-demand of work, that oh so constant reminder that without slaving away in exchange for those thin little pieces of paper with someone's picture printed on them (money), you would wind up hungry and eventually even homeless. With taxes to pay; kids to raise and educate; cars and houses and yards to maintain; groceries to buy; clothes to wear; and of course, toys to play with, etcetera, work is one of those inevitables that seems to fully eclipsed our everyday choices. It's not like we can say, "I am choosing a different path in life, one that is devoid of work," but rather it is a matter of "No work, no pay. No pay, no food, clothing or shelter."

There has been much research conducted and data collected by both governments as well as private institutions on what is termed a time use survey (TUS). I am not going to discuss the results of these studies, as everyone's time schedule is different, yet no doubt pretty much consumed in responsibilities. The net result for most, however, is that there's no time left for something as abstract-sounding as "Spending serious time in the pursuit of a friendship with a God that no one has seen!

I will, however, share a few of the headings or time-categories as used by the US Bureau of Labor Statistics. In their surveys, they break time into the following categories, of which categories I list here only for the purpose of helping you recall what voraciously consumes your days.

They group activities as well as subgroups as follows:

▶ **Personal Care Activities**
    Sleeping
    Eating and drinking
▶ **Household Activities**
    Housework
    Food preparation and cleanup
    Lawn and garden care
▶ **Household management**
    Purchasing goods and services
    Consumer goods purchases
▶ **Professional and personal care services**
    Caring for and helping household members
    Caring for and helping household children
    Caring for and helping non-household members
    Caring for and helping non-household adults
▶ **Working and work-related Activities**
    Working
▶ **Educational Activities**
    Attending class
    Homework and research
▶ **Organizational, Civic, and Religious Activities**
    Religious and spiritual activities
    Volunteering (organizational and civic activities)
▶ **Leisure and sports**
    Socializing and communicating
    Watching television
    Participating in sports, exercise, and recreation
    Telephone calls, mail, and e-mail.

The point is, that amid all the demands of the 24-hour time-allotment called a day, where are you going to carve out a time slot for Jesus? Given the above information, the question is, "How exactly does one put Jesus first?"

At this point, it may be of supportive revelation to take a look at human relationship development as a means of helping us to garner an understanding of what it takes to create a solid bond of friendship. More specifically, how about using dating and courtship as a means of comparison and contrast?

Imagine that you are in the midst of an intense courtship with the girl or boy of your dreams and, for all intensive purposes, you know that he or she is "the one"—the relevant question should be: how do you get across to that person that they are truly number one in your life, that is, they are the number one on your list of your priorities? Is it accomplished by giving them a quick two minute phone call (prayer) once a day to say "I love you," and then on the weekend arrange to block out a couple of hours of time (church) for a date? Can you simply skip all the time spent and throw a few gifts their way, flowers, chocolates, gift certificates, etcetera? Or how about skipping the time and the gifts and just letting them know that although the two of you don't see each other much, you let everyone else know that you are in love with only them and that should suffice in showing commitment?

I really don't think so. If a romantic relationship wouldn't be possible with little- effort expended, how could one possibly be so naive as to think it might work in the development of a relationship with a jealous-for-us God?

So how much time spent is enough to create a dynamic relationship with Jesus? Or is this even a legitimate question when looking at the pursuit of a Savior who gave His all in order to win our hearts? Unfortunately, the very question itself is fraught with dichotomy from its very pronouncement as it infers the pursuit of some minimum. You see, the question, "How much is enough?" is inherently aimed at finding some imaginary line of the minimum amount of seeking required in order to "find."

Thus, in light of everything written in the Bible, both hints as well as bold factual statements, regarding what it takes to secure and maintain a dividend paying relationship with Jesus, we find that it is an all or nothing pursuit on our part that directly leads to an either all or nothing relationship.

So is it even possible to quantify what a passionate pursuit of Jesus may look like against the backdrop of the categories of life-demand as laid out above?

As I expressed in the early chapters of this book, through revealing my own personal experience, the only deal that I ever cut with God that actually produced some form of measurable dividend was that of offering time rather than tithes, offerings or nice words. It was only when I chose to carve out a one-hour block of my busy schedule each and every early morning, that I was finally able to experience, in even a small way, a real connection with a Savior I could not visually see nor physically touch.

The Hour of Power

I am often asked the question: Why an hour a day? Where did that come from? First, let me be clear, it isn't about "works" nor a formula that magically produces a relationship. Rather it is about giving a budding spiritual "romance" time to develop into something deeper. I have received more than my fair share of criticism, sometimes by prominent theologians, who have stated that my challenge—"If you don't spend at least an hour a day with Jesus then don't expect a dynamic relationship with Him"—is basically a message of righteousness by works. Well, based on my personal experience as well as the experiences of literally thousands of others who have put into practice this resolution, my response is, "Call it what you like, in fact, go ahead and label it 'works'—all I know is that it works."

The point is, a relationship doesn't happen because God has some magical formula, which, if we follow, we will somehow be rewarded with a miraculous connection with our Savior. Rather, it is through engaging in daily, serious time together, where passion can begin to develop, just as one would in through the courtship mentioned above. If the Holy Spirit is to teach us all things than it behooves us to spend a serious amount of time in the "classroom" of communion with our Lord and Savior so that both lessons and relationship can develop and flourish.

In regard to spending time each day with Jesus and consequently opening ourselves up to being taught, we must recognize a significantly noteworthy fact, that one of the job descriptions of the Holy Spirit is, "he shall teach you all things" (John 14:26). If that is truly the case, then it behooves us to consider attending classes on a daily basis so that adequate time is given for the instructor to instruct. It is no different when we relate it to that of formally attending school. Who on this planet could honestly suggest that it is possible to not attend your twelve or so years of basic education and still come out the other side having somehow learned the lessons that need to be learned? No time spent with the teacher, no learning gained. It is imperative that we follow the mandate of the Holy Bible, that of passionately seeking Jesus through time spent together if we are to ever hope to be party to a meaningful relationship with Him.

In relating to this particular discussion and as mentioned above, I have many times been asked why did I choose the time increment of one hour? Why not fifteen minutes, or a half an hour. Or maybe even all day long in Bible study and prayer?

Well, first and foremost I had, in the past, tried the smaller time increments of study and prayer (10 or 20 minutes) and, for some reason, I was unable to settle into that zone where the world around me seemed to vanish from view and I was left feeling connected to something of great power and significance. So, obviously, I wasn't about to try the same thing twice and hope for better results. And, second, on rare occasions I must add, I had heard or read the success formulas of several different stalwart of faith-type people who recommended a "thoughtful hour each day in contemplation of the life of Jesus" as a sure means of connecting with the Savior.

One such comes from Mother Teresa, who stated, "Spend one hour a day in adoration of the Lord and you'll be all right." What she meant by the phrase "all right," I am not a hundred percent sure, but I am dead sure that her life was a depiction of what everyone's lives should look like if they are truly pursuing Jesus with a passion. This little Catholic woman gave up all worldly gain and status in order to allow none-other than Jesus to touch the lives of the least in society and, in doing so, she met face to face with her Savior every day of her life. You see, contained within the passage of Matthew 25:31–46 is the clear statement that "I was hungry" and you either fed me or you chose not to. "I was thirsty" and you either gave me drink or you chose not to, etcetera.

Jesus is delivering here a gigantic hint of monumental proportion—a hint that will fulfill one of those probable thoughts we may have harbored in the past. The thought being, how many of us have ever wished that we could catch even a small glimpse of Jesus—maybe in a nighttime dream or even a daytime vision?

I had always thought that my faith would be greatly bolstered if I could only see what Jesus looked like or, if not what He looked like, to just simply be privy to see something like a silhouetted image against a bright shining light. I guess I am sort of like Philip was where, in John 14:8, 9, he admits that his curiosity was mounting while at the same time his faith in the visually unseen was waning. "Philip said to Him, 'Lord, show us the Father, and it is sufficient for us.' Jesus said to him, 'Have I been with you so long, and yet you have not known Me, Philip? He who has seen Me has seen the Father; so how can you say, 'Show us the Father'?'"

Jesus here diverts Philip's attention from the direction he was headed to that of a completely different focus. The Master, in essence, was simply saying, "I am having a hard time understanding your need to look beyond what you are seeing everyday as you travel with me. If you have seen me, then you have seen the Father."

Interestingly, when I, like Phillip, ask Jesus today, "Please let me physically see you so that my faith can become stronger?" He similarly replies with, "I," not someone else, "am hungry" and you are either willing to feed me and thus see me face-to-face or you are going to choose to reject me and thus will go on through life wishing you could someday catch a visual glimpse of me." In other words, "inasmuch as you did it to one of the least of these . . . you did it to Me" (Matthew 25:40).

According to this passage, Mother Teresa would have probably been more familiar with what Jesus looked like, in the figurative, then any contemporary person I know or have heard of. She, after all, "sold all that she had" in order to pursue that one pearl of great price as talked of in Matthew 13:45, 46 where it states: "Again, the kingdom of heaven is like a merchant seeking beautiful pearls, who, when he had found one pearl of great price, went and sold all that he had and bought it." So after hearing of her recommendation, as well as a couple of other stalwarts of faith, I was led to a new standard of what seeking might actually look like and I, therefore, chose an hour a day as my level of pursuit towards a relationship with Jesus.

Tithing of Time

It may sound a bit abstract but along these same lines of reasoning, I had come to the conclusion a number of years ago that the stewardship sermons ("Bring your tithes and offerings in order to be blessed") that I was accustomed to hearing from the pulpit were featuring one of the lesser priorities to God. It dawned on me one day that when the Bible states that we should tithe our assets to the level of 10 percent, as found in Leviticus 27:32 and other places "And concerning the tithe of the herd or the flock, of whatever passes under the rod, the tenth one shall be holy to the Lord") that quite possibly God has distributed other assets to us, other than paper dollar bills, that should also be tithed. After spending much time studying the subject of Biblical stewardship in its truest sense, I came to the conclusion that a more complete list of God-given assets to be tithed is as follows as well as being ordered in what I would consider of greatest to least priority to God: time, talent, energy, and money.

Time: Whether we choose to consider it or not, we have all been allotted a certain amount of time in which to cram a "life's-worth" of living into. The Bible states that we, post-antediluvian people, can expect an average lifespan of approximately seventy years (Psalm 90:10) in which to procreate and do whatever it is that we are going to do with our lives. Obviously, some live much longer and some tragically live considerably less. The point is, we have all been given a gift of a bit of time to live, and we are definitely accountable as to how we should invest it.

Talent: Whether all agree or not, everyone one of us has been given some measure of talent in which, and on which, to build careers, hobbies, and/or ministries for God. We are told, through the parable of the talents (Matthew 25:14–30), that we are accountable to God for the development of whatever asset God has given us and as such, we cannot let it or them fade away without an inherent, negative consequence.

Energy: Since the ability to push our productivity in life is very much dependent on the health and subsequent energy we are given from which to draw, we need to apportion that asset over a whole list of demands, not the least of which is work, relationship development, and play. It you do not comprehend just how valuable an asset, energy is, then simply spend some time visiting the dying in your local hospital. You will be made aware of how blessed you really are.

Money: No explanation is even needed to understand both the value of money to our society as well as how easy it is to waste it on frivolity.

Of the four assets briefly outlined above, it must be understood that the one of greatest value to God is not the one that we, as money-dependent Christians, talk most of—tithing. No, we are more than informed that God already owns absolutely everything on, and including, this planet (see Psalm 50:10; 1 Corinthians 10:26; Haggai 2:8; 1 Chronicles 29:12–14; Job 41:11), so He obviously isn't dependent on us for money. Rather, the greatest gift we can return to God in the form of a tithe, if you will, is that of the precious time He has so willingly granted us in the first place. To invest a portion of that time into developing a relationship with Jesus as well as into sharing the gospel of this same Jesus with a hungry and broken world, is the one asset that will pay the greatest dividends to the kingdom of heaven itself.

If we were to try to figure out what a ten percent tithe would look like in terms of time invested in Jesus and His cause, we simply need to look at our waking and non-waking minutes in any given day and then do the calculations. If we were to look at tithing ten percent, at a minimum, of our whole allotment of a 24 hour (1,440 minutes) day, we would be returning to Jesus, 144 minutes or 2.4 hours a day. If we choose to look only at the conservative minimum, that of our waking hours of approximately 17 hours (1,020 minutes), our time investment in Jesus would be 102 minutes or 1.7 hours per day.

The point of it all? To then look at the bottom line of considering time a valuable asset to be, in essence, tithed for Jesus, a one-hour per day investment in Jesus is basically an investment in the realm of "short-changing" God and therefore not to be considered an overly generous gift nor aggressive investment.

Diversions

Again along the lines of tithing time, few statements have ever stuck in my mind like the one I heard an old radio evangelist named Joe Crews once make. I heard him make this statement at a point probably seven or eight years before my "born-again" experience. Admittedly, at the time I had concluded that the guy was an out-of-touch, ultra-conservative, legalist. Nevertheless, his words burned their own little place of storage in my brain. He simply stated this: "If you spend more time watching television than you do on your knees and in the Bible, you can't possibly make it to Heaven."

Looking back now, and in light of what the Bible clearly teaches about making Jesus number one in our lives, it is probably one of the most accurate and relevant statements anyone could ever make in an attempt to impart what it means to "Seek ye first" Jesus.

Yes, it may fit the category of being a little politically incorrect and maybe even step on a few, if not a myriad, of toes but the evidence is there to tell us that television generally inhabits the number one position in the priority list of the average person in modern society. One only needs to look at the statistics on TV watching to realize that it consumes a massive amount our available time in life and therefore truly is the number one, non-essential pursuit in life.

Referencing the Nielson Company's November 2008 "A2/M2 Three Screen Report," we find that the average person in the US watches approximately 142 hours of TV a month. Those with Internet spend 27 hours per month on it; and those with the capable mobile phones spend an average of three hours per month watching mobile videos. Put into ugly perspective, that means that the average American will spend 3.5 months of their waking, non-sleep hours per year in full time television viewing; or, in other words, they will spend approximately 19 years of a 65 year life devoted exclusively to watching TV.

And we wonder sometimes what the scriptural reference Matthew 6:24 actually means? "No one can serve two masters; for either he will hate the one and love the other, or else he will be loyal to the one and despise the other. You cannot serve God and mammon."

The three screens reported on, being that of television, internet and mobile phone, clearly consume the bulk, if not all, of the average person's available spare time. Such consumption of our time is in direct competition with that of the time we should be both spending with families as well as, more importantly, in pursuit of our Lord and Savior, Jesus. If Jesus is to actually be put number one, in terms of our pursuit, our interest as well as our love, then it only makes sense to believe that Jesus will be entitled the greatest portion of our non-obligatory working, sleeping and eating time. Put in simple terms, if, on any given day, you spend maybe a two-hour block of time watching TV, surfing the net, or text messaging, etcetera and you spend only an hour in pursuit of Jesus, through prayer and Bible study, then you clearly and unequivocally are not "seeking first" Jesus but rather, seeking first that which is offered by the world.

Satan's greatest weapon against the God-spirituality of us humans is that of stealing time away from our relationship building with Jesus. I can only imagine Satan's glee when we are made aware of the effects of the bad influence of TV on our spiritual characters, which are to be keen to the still small voice of the Holy Spirit, and respond by clicking the channel to some mindless, brain-dead sitcom, complete with canned laughing in the background. He knows we are going to eventually stumble across the negative statistics, and he is completely fine with that as long as we just shift our viewing addiction onto something else, less violent, yet time-burning.

Priorities thus, I ask: Do we actually wonder why we don't see the miracles taking place today as was portrayed through the lives of the early church disciples in the book of Acts? Could it be that because there are very few, if any, self-proclaimed Christians today who truly place Jesus number one on the time, talent, energy and money list of priorities of their lives that that may have something to do with the lack of the divinely miraculous in our present day churches? In light of the warning of Matthew 24:37–39 aligning the times to that of Noah before the Flood, could there be a correlation between only eight people being righteous enough to get on board the ark and the proportionate number of righteous today when the two eras of Biblical history are paralleled?

It is a sobering thought to consider that, biblically, there is no such thing as securing a relationship with Jesus until such time as we decide He is actually worth the effort that we would put into our number one priority in life. Luke 12:34 pretty much sums it up: "For where your treasure is, there your heart will be also." If one hour out of a twenty-four hour day is considered too much of an inconvenience to what is really important to us then, quite simply, why would you ever fully expect to have God answer when you call for help? You are, in essence, calling out to someone you don't know, nor does He know you.

Again, I quote Matthew 7:21–23: "Not everyone who says to Me, 'Lord, Lord,' shall enter the kingdom of heaven, but he who does the will of My Father in heaven. Many will say to Me in that day,

'Lord, Lord, have we not prophesied in Your name, cast out demons in Your name, and done many wonders in Your name?' And then I will declare to them, 'I never knew you; depart from Me, you who practice lawlessness!' "In light of this reference of subliminal warning, as well as many others, there should be no surprises whatsoever when we, the TV-watching, Internet-surfing, mobile-phone-texting, generation are left to wonder, "Why is God so quiet these days?"

Jesus in the Garden

As I have mentioned, my choice of an hour a day as a starting point was predicated on both the advice of those I considered as spiritual giants, as well as a reference made in Matthew 26. It is a chapter that records the agony that Jesus went through in the garden of Gethsemane as the full realization of what was about to happen began to weigh heavily on His mind. It references His need and dependence on His human friends, especially their intercessory prayers on His behalf, as well as their need to be spiritually connected for what was about to come.

After having spent time alone praying to His Father, comes back to the three disciples, only to find them asleep. Here we observe the only time increment exposed in the gospels as to what the private "seeking" of Jesus may actually look like. It is found in Matthew 26:40 where it states, "Then He came to the disciples and found them sleeping, and said to Peter, 'What! Could you not watch with Me one hour?'"

Through the way Jesus makes this statement, we are led to believe that the one hour suggested was that of a minimum increment of time spent in prayer, not a time allotment that He had pre-arranged, or agreed-to, with them. The assumption portrayed here is that of (paraphrased with liberties), "I can't believe that you are so oblivious as to what is about to happen, Peter, that you don't feel it necessary to spend even one hour in prayer."

Upon making this statement, Jesus then continues with an alternate reason for His request that they spend a serious amount of time in prayer. Verse 41: "Watch and pray, lest you enter into temptation. The spirit indeed is willing, but the flesh is weak." In essence, Jesus is warning them that to not spend a serious amount of time in prayer will inherently leave one defenseless and susceptible to being overcome in the battle against Satan and his powers of darkness. Since prayer is the link to Heaven, and we are pawns in the great controversy brewing between the God of love and His bullying detractor, it becomes critical, for our own salvation, to remain as connected as we can throughout our day.

Who, as a soldier fighting in a battle (because that is what we are) would not find comfort, advantage and strength in being given the option of maintaining constant radio communication with one's commanding officer? Especially since that Officer has the enemy under constant surveillance and knows its every move—all in addition to the fact that the Officer has already defeated the enemy two thousand years ago through the death of His own son in a battle of all battles?

Who could possibly misunderstand that the "seek" part of finding a dynamic relationship with Jesus is not about "works" or some "paint-by-numbers" formula, but rather about time spent with the love of one's life? Isn't about enjoying a courtship of quiet times together, of slowly, over much time spent, getting to know each other, of laughing and crying together, all the while growing deeper and deeper in love?

A Marriage Made in Heaven

The Bible itself uses the parallel of marriage as an example of what a relationship with God will look like. Isaiah 62:5 is just one example of such analogy where it states: "As the bridegroom rejoices over the bride, so shall your God rejoice over you." Anyone with one ounce of discernment will understand and recognize that the discovery time during courtship is not only necessary, in order to determine compatibility, but rewarding and of natural desire.

Although it is true that time investment is of absolute necessity, there is also another element that is imperative as well, that of there must be some level of passion invested. Of course we are not talking of the passion of sexual pursuit but rather the passion of extreme interest. Without that element, there will be no indication divulged to the other person that the pursuit of a love-relationship is actually "in the air."

In human terms, at a minimum, each party to a budding relationship needs to know that they are the number one desire of their dating partner in order for a relationship to steadily and securely grow into a period of formal engagement followed by the lifelong bond of indestructible marriage.

The entire process of getting to know Jesus is not meant to be burdensome or labor intensive. Rather, it is about something beautiful and meaningful. Jesus wants us to know that, contrary to Satan's misrepresentations, He is not only approachable and desirous of a courtship and marriage with us, but also that the relationship building time is going to be a joyous and rewarding experience.

In Matthew 11:28–30 Jesus beautifully divulges the process of "coming to Him" as something akin to an extreme positive, not a negative experience—certainly not one of works and labor. He states: "Come to Me, all you who labor and are heavy laden, and I will give you rest. Take My yoke upon you and learn from Me, for I am gentle and lowly in heart, and you will find rest for your souls. For My yoke is easy and My burden is light."

Exposed within the words of this passage are many hints as to what is in store for us if we choose to be in a deep relationship with Him.

First, Jesus wants us to know that He understands our plight in this world, that life is full of toil and disappointment. He knows the perpetual pressure we feel when we are pretty much forced into competing in society's unfulfilling rat race. After all, no one ever seems to win anyhow as we simply spin our wheels with no forward progress seemingly observable. And, second, Jesus divulges the idea that to engage in a pursuit of Him is going to result in your being granted one of the most elusive states of being found on this planet, that of a genuine rest and peace-of-mind. Most of us can barely comprehend what it would be like to be able to truly cast off all care and worry and simply allow the gentle breeze of tranquility to engulf our tattered beings. With Jesus, relationship building is all about benefit to us since that is what true love is all about anyhow. He wants us to know that He is all about "peace" and "rest." He makes that point doubly clear in John 14:27, where He states: "Peace I leave with you, My peace I give to you; not as the world gives do I give to you. Let not your heart be troubled, neither let it be afraid."

Jesus next continues explaining what the process of courtship will be like. He tells us to put on His "yoke," which can connote only one thing: that we will be engaged in some form of pursuit or work. But in case someone may jump to a quick conclusion that they don't like the connotation of work as a means of relationship building, Jesus, at the end of this passage, clarifies what that work will actually be like by stating, "For my yoke is easy, and my burden is light." He also adds that part of that work, or pursuit-process, will be to learn of Him.

It only makes sense to compare this with what results in human courtship between a couple in love. By spending a serious amount of impassioned time together in pursuit of each other, they quite naturally learn more of each other. And just so we don't ever envision that to attempt to develop a relationship with the Son of God is going to be a strange abstract process, Jesus tells us exactly what we will find on the other end of our pursuit of Him. He tells us that we are going to find a gentle and loving partner, not one of arrogance and lofty stature. He simply states: "I am meek and lowly in heart." In other words, He is not only extremely approachable but He is humble, unassuming and very ready to accept and reward your pursuit of Him.

In conclusion, there are no short cuts to developing a relationship with Jesus, just as there are no known shortcuts to securing a deep relationship with someone special of the opposite sex. I can very comfortably advocate that if you want the dynamic relationship with Jesus, and in doing so, He is perceived as even mildly worth some effort, then you are going to spend at least one hour a day in pursuit of Him. I can absolutely guarantee results for two rock-solid reasons.

One, God Himself delivers the bulletproof promise of, "Seek and you will [not, might] find"; and two, personal testimony is of paramount value in assessing results. Through my own experience, as well as the literally hundreds of emails, letters and calls I am blessed to receive from all parts of the world, the "hour of power" (as some have now coined it) continues to change and transform lives.

Simply put, if Jesus can't occupy one twenty-fourth of your day, every day, then quite frankly, you really don't want Him in the first place. Although you may desire the benefits of an association with Him, if time for Him is too much of a sacrifice against the reward of a personal relationship, then you're simply walking down a dead-end street where Jesus does not live nor will He ever be found.

CHAPTER 12

THE FINAL STEP

AVING JUST DISCOVERED THE CLEAR MEANS OF BOTH finding and maintaining a viable and vibrant relationship with Jesus, I ask you, *What does it take to put sizzle into your courtship and "marriage" with Jesus?* In other words, this is the third and final step, and without it, your ever-growing relationship with the divine will slowly wither and die.

Faithful in the Large and the Small

Matthew 7:20 starts us off. We are told that there has to be some very observable signs that a relationship even exists in the first place. "Therefore by their fruits you will know them." In other words, not only you but also others will be able to readily observe that you have a real relationship with a results-producing God. There will be unmistakable manifestations of the connection you have with Jesus.

As we discovered earlier, God has a standard by which a relationship with Him can be measured, and through which others will observe, that is beyond anything we can even fathom or imagine.

Mark 16:17, 18 states: "And these signs will follow those who believe: In My name they will cast out demons; they will speak with new tongues; they will take up serpents; and if they drink anything deadly, it will by no means hurt them; they will lay hands on the sick, and they will recover."

Even though as a brand new creature in Jesus, you may not observe miracles of this level, there will most definitely emerge "mini" responsibilities and miracles that will begin to permeate your life. Your dedication and surrender is key, and if you seek His face daily, if you remain faithful to His call, you will see miracles. In Matthew 25:21 Jesus uses a parable to disclose both the test of faithfulness as well as the reward of greater responsibility through that faithfulness. He simply summarizes by stating: "His lord said to him, Well done, good and faithful servant; you were faithful over a few things, I will make you ruler over many things. Enter into the joy of your lord."

Quite clearly, you can't expect the big miracles when you can't be trusted with the little responsibilities that Jesus places before you. It is the same way with the blessings promised in Deuteronomy 28:1–14. If you seek the blessing ahead of the God who bestows them, then you will never taste the blessing. It is only when we seek the Blessor ahead of the blessings that it is possible to experience the said blessings. It must be understood that there is a reason and purpose for each of our lives here on planet earth. We can discover part of that purpose by looking at the great commission given us in Matthew 28:19 where it commands, "Go therefore and make disciples of all the nations, baptizing them in the name of the Father and of the Son and of the Holy Spirit."

By engaging ourselves in process of evangelism—any of a myriad forms of outreach—and thereby fulfilling God's greatest need of our lives, we will be setting ourselves up to be privy to observing miracles galore. We will discover both the miracle of watching lost souls find joy and relevance in their lives as well as the miraculous transformation that will take place in our own lives.

You see, Jesus' parable of the vine and branches found in John 15—where there is an observable, fruit-producing result of a branch being intimately connected with the vine—inherently exposes the miraculous. There exists an unmistakable cause and effect of being connected with the Savior. Matthew 13:23 even quantifies the result of that connection by way of the parable of the Sower sowing seeds. "But he who received seed on the good ground is he who hears the word and understands it, who indeed bears fruit and produces: some a hundredfold, some sixty, some thirty."

When this verse talks of the fruit bearing expected it actually puts a number on what the results may look like. Some will bring forth a hundred, some sixty and some thirty. The mere fact that a number is suggested here means that there should be some observable output of the life that is connected with Jesus.

Of course, when one considers that the entire gospel of Jesus Christ can be summarized in the four simple words—"Not I but Christ" (Galatians 2:20)—we will be quickly led to the realization that, for anything to happen in our lives, it is going to have to be performed by a power outside of ourselves. And that power, of course, is Jesus.

How, then, does one become the "conduit" or pipe through which Jesus will do His magnificent work in and through us?

The Submission of Self

In James 4:7, he answers that question like this: "Therefore submit to God." James is telling us that there is something we must do in order to fulfill the gospel's summary, again, that of "not I but Christ." We are to "submit" or relinquish control of our lives to the God of the Universe and, thus, allow His power to flow through us. It is only by abandoning our carnal ways, which, in essence, are polluted with self-motivation and self-interest, that we will ever fully taste and possess the truly relevant life promised in the Bible.

Unfortunately, as we discovered in the unveiling of the first two steps, this may sound simple and straightforward until we look at it in the full context of the rest of the Bible. It is admittedly easy sometimes to simply buy into a statement from the Bible and then apply what we consider to be just enough effort to legitimize such statement; it is quite another, on the other hand, to accept the full intent as expressed in the Bible. By nature, we most often learn to apply only the bare minimum to fulfill our obligations in life simply because there is so much that is demanded of us already.

The trouble for us, when it pertains to the Bible and biblical principles, is that there is no such thing as a short cut to spiritual success when it relates to having and retaining a relationship with our Creator, Jesus

Jesus, Our Example

For starters, it is vitally important to first look at Jesus, our example. 1 John 2:6 states, "He who says he abides in Him ought himself also to walk just as He walked." States 1 Peter 2:21, "Christ also suffered for us, leaving us an example, that you should follow His steps."

If we are to use Jesus as our example or mentor, then we must look at how Jesus submitted to His Father in order for us to become aware of our obligation.

First, I must clarify a point that had eluded me most of my "religious" life. Is it really a fair comparison to use Jesus as an example when He was somehow able to live a completely sinless life? I used to quietly harbor the thought that it wasn't a fair comparison since I believed that, although Jesus took on full humanity, He had maintained a little divinity for use when things got tough. Yes, I believed that for the most part He was human but there was that little element of cynicism that plagued my thoughts. How could it be a fair comparison when He had to have kept a little divinity tucked in His back pocket, so to speak?

Fortunately for me, this thought found its way into the garbage bin of my misconceptions when, years later, I began a fervent study of the book of John, which showed me so clearly that everything Jesus did came from the Father, not from Himself. In John 6:38, Jesus broadcasts the news as to what His agenda was when He left Heaven to come to this decrepit planet. He stated: "For I have come down from heaven, not to do My own will, but the will of Him who sent Me." The essence of what Jesus is saying can most adequately be summarized in the short phrase, "Not I, but my Father."

As we discovered earlier, the summary of our spiritual existence looks familiar through the gospel's very summary, that of "Not I but Christ" (Galatians 2:20). Clearly, Jesus chose no human advantage in life but rather fully gave His life up to be used by His Father. In order for us to observe just what that dependence on His Father actually looks like, we can turn to what I consider to be the single most powerful chapter in the book of John, that of chapter 14. In John 14:10 Jesus states that "the Father who dwells in Me does the works." And to make sure we clearly get the point, we also read in verse 24 that "the word which you hear is not Mine but the Father's who sent Me."

In terms of using His own human power, Jesus wanted to make it abundantly clear that He didn't do, of Himself, any of the incredible stuff that we normally attribute to Him but that it all came directly from the Father, albeit, through Him.

It is absolutely critical that we allow this point to sink deep, as it opens the door to the liberating reality that Jesus fully expects to perform the same, if not greater, works through us as His Father did through Him. (Reference, John 14:12: "Most assuredly, I say to you, he who believes in Me, the works that I do he will do also; and greater works than these he will do, because I go to My Father.") It was for that reason that Jesus went to such great lengths to try to get us to understand that the source of power and agenda was not His alone, but rather the will of His Father. The power or juice that He tapped into was most definitely an external, not an internal source.

Jesus and the Father

As we allow ourselves to focus more closely on the concept of Jesus as our example, it is imperative that we seek to understand the level of submission entered into when Jesus, in the garden of Gethsemane, struggled with the reality of the horrific experience that was about to happen to Him. We can sense both the extreme agony He went through as well as the release of burden He felt in giving up on His own agenda. The biblical account very graphically exposes the battle that was tormenting our Savior's mind where in Matthew 26:39 it states: "He went a little farther and fell on His face, and prayed, saying, "O My Father, if it is possible, let this cup pass from Me; nevertheless, not as I will, but as You will."

Here, amid horrific anguish, we find Jesus completely emptying Himself of His own desires and agenda and basically handing all over to His Father. He let us see what it means to submit one's will to someone else, so that when it came to our choice to submit, we would be able to understand the level of such submission.

In John 5:19 He makes this point abundantly clear by stating: "Then Jesus answered and said to them, "Most assuredly, I say to you, the Son can do nothing of Himself, but what He sees the Father do; for whatever He does, the Son also does in like manner." Jesus chose to impart to us an understanding of the parallel between "ourselves in relation to Him" and "Himself in relation to His Father." In John 15:5 we read that "without me [Jesus] you can do nothing." This point should be easy to grasp because who doesn't understand that there is nothing in the human arsenal of talents and gifts that would ever qualify us to initiate any kind of a supernatural act. The reality of human life is that we are pretty much limited to the use of brawn, brains and words—period.

It is an entirely different thought, though, to believe that Jesus, the Son of God, in human flesh, also had to rely solely on the power of His Father. It is a point of great importance if we are to truly believe that Jesus can and should be our example as to how we should run our lives. It was for this reason that in John 5, Jesus fleshes out the parallel between Himself and us by stating, in verse 30, "I can of Myself do nothing." He desired that we see how it worked between Himself and His Father so that we would ultimately have an understanding of how it should work between Him and ourselves.

Hidden within this same verse 30, we find another related and pertinent point. Jesus said, "I do not seek My own will but the will of the Father who sent Me." To add supportive depth to this point, we can also look at John 4:34. "Jesus said to them, "My food is to do the will of Him who sent Me, and to finish His work."

Lights to the World

Clearly Jesus' role was principally that of being a conduit through which His Father could expose His deep love and compassion to a broken world. Because of this example and because we are to follow in Jesus' footsteps, we, also surrendering ourselves, can reveal that same unconditional love and compassion to others as well. Each and every one of us share one thing in common, we were and are ordained to reveal God the way that Jesus Himself did. This truth is powerfully exposed in the book of John, through a rather interesting series of statements and proclamations by Jesus, Himself.

It says, referring to John the Baptist, in John 1:6, 7 that "There was a man sent from God, whose name was John. This man came for a witness, to bear witness of the Light, that all through him might believe." What should stand out as more than a bit strange, though, is the content of the very next statement, that of "He was not that Light" (John 1:8).

"Strange?" Because why state the obvious. Of course we know that John the Baptist was not the light, after all, what knowledgeable Christian doesn't know who the light of the world is? John 8:12 being one such reference of statement of fact: "Then Jesus spoke to them again, saying, 'I am the light of the world.'"Who could argue with a statement so categorically factual as to leave absolutely no doubt whatsoever?

However, my deeper study brought out a crucial point. Jesus started adding qualifiers or subjects to his statement of categorical fact. It was no longer simply, "I am the light of the world," but rather that statement began to evolve into a different meaning and direction. One chapter later in John 9:5 we read Jesus' own words again. This time though, he puts a condition on His statement. He states, "As long as I am in the world, I am the light of the world." By adding the qualifier "as long as I am in the world" to the statement "I am the light of the world," Jesus is, in essence, subliminally breaking the potentially scary news to us that when He leaves and is no longer here, He will no longer be the light. You see if Jesus is the light only when He is physically present with us here on this earth then the connotation is that of when He leaves, He will most definitely no longer be the light.

The question that should immediately come to mind is that of, "What is going to happen to us, post-Jesus' death-and-resurrection people? Are we going to be left in the dark, without a light? Will a new form of light be given, like maybe that of the Holy Spirit becoming our light in addition to also being our teacher (John 14:26)?

Moving on chronologically, we find another hint as to what is about to happen to the "light of the world" as we know it. In John 12:35 we read: "Then Jesus said to them, A little while longer the light is with you. Walk while you have the light, lest darkness overtake you; he who walks in darkness does not know where he is going." It is important to note that this is again Jesus speaking of Himself. The mere fact that Jesus puts a time limitation on Him being the "light" indicates, without doubt, that He is no longer going to be the "light of the world" once He leaves and returns to Heaven.

We first hear Jesus, with pointed emphasis, boldly telling us that none other than He is the sole "the light of the world." He then modifies that statement quite drastically by adding a qualifier, "as long as I am in the world, I am the light." Following that He then adds another twist, that of "in a short period of time you won't have me as your light anymore." Jesus has made it a point to gently break the news to us that we are not to expect Him, at least in the flesh, to continue as the source of light on this earth.

Now, added to this strange series of progressive statements, we hear Jesus add another interesting statement of fact. It can be found in John 16:7, where He states: "Nevertheless I tell you the truth. It is to your advantage that I go away." Why would Jesus say that? Why would He say that it is for our benefit that He leaves sooner rather than later? Fortunately, verse 7 doesn't end there but continues with these words: "For if I do not go away, the Helper will not come to you; but if I depart, I will send Him to you." Does that mean that the Comforter, or the Holy Spirit, is now going to show up and replace Jesus as our new light? One may be inclined to think that but it is important that we back up and look at what happened when John the Baptist, the one who was not the light, baptized Jesus.

We can read the account in John 1:29–32 where it states, "The next day John saw Jesus coming toward him, and said, 'Behold! The Lamb of God who takes away the sin of the world! This is He of whom I said, "After me comes a Man who is preferred before me, for He was before me." I did not know Him; but that He should be revealed to Israel, therefore I came baptizing with water.' And John bore witness, saying, I saw the Spirit descending from heaven like a dove, and He remained upon Him."

We are here given an account of Jesus' baptism by water immersion but, more importantly, we see something else. John the Baptist makes an observation of monumental importance. He states that "I saw the Spirit descending from heaven like a dove, and He remained upon Him." Obviously, the Spirit here is none other than that of the Holy Spirit. Jesus was both baptized with water as well as the Holy Spirit. What is significant here is the fact that there is a parallel going on between us and that of Jesus. We cannot overlook the fact that as we read in John 16:7, Jesus stated He needed to leave as quickly as possible so that the something important could take place. That, of course, was so that He could send the Holy Spirit on us, just as His Father in Heaven had sent the Holy Spirit on Him.

We now need to ask an extremely important question. Is the Holy Spirit the new light? No, it can't be since Jesus made it clear that He was the light. So what then is the role of the Holy Spirit?

To answer that question, lets first look at it as it pertains to Jesus' experience with being anointed by the Holy Spirit. It is important to note the point at which Jesus' formal ministry actually began. It was at the point of His baptism, specifically the baptism of the Holy Spirit—the dove that descended from Heaven upon Him. Prior to that, Jesus was a carpenter by trade. After that, Jesus became a minister for His Father. Prior to Jesus' baptism, He was not the light. After His baptism, Jesus became both a minister for His Father as well as, and more importantly, He became "the light of the world." So it is the anointing of the Holy Spirit that makes the recipient of that anointing, the light; it is not the Holy Spirit being the light through the recipient.

With that little bit of background, let us now move to why Jesus would have said that it is for our benefit that He leaves in an expedited way. He desperately wanted to leave quickly for one gigantic reason, that of shedding His previous role as light of the world and bestowing that honor on us through the same anointing of the Holy Spirit. Yes, it is titillating true, we, post death and resurrection people, are the new "light of the world." I say "post-death-and-resurrection people" because those on the other side of the cross including John the Baptist, as great as he was (Matthew 11:11), were not "the light of the world."

Something monumental happened. Jesus came to this earth, lived a sinless life as proof that full submission to the Father will give you victory. He was anointed to become the light of the world; ministered and then died on a cruel cross so that you and I could become lights to the world. Jesus' death and following resurrection from the grave earned back the dominion of the world from Satan's icy grip and as a result legitimized Jesus' right to appoint us as His heir apparent.

Parallels

What proof is there that that is what took place and what continues to take place?

The answer can be found in John 17, where we hear Jesus praying to His Father for those that we lead to Him through our witness—"I do not pray for these alone, but also for those who will believe in Me through their word" (verse 20). Most importantly, we see the parallel between the role Jesus' played to His Father as well as our role to Jesus. In John 17:18 Jesus says, "As You sent Me into the world, I also have sent them into the world." Here Jesus is comparing His working relationship with His Father with that of our working relationship with Him. He wants to make sure we understand that the same role that He played with His Father is also to be our role with Him. Here is the punch line to the whole thing. Clearly, Jesus was sent into this world, with the anointing of the Holy Spirit at the time of His baptism, to fulfill the role of being the light of this cold, dark world.

Now that He is in heaven, He is seeking us, His people, to be lights to the world. Just as Jesus was sent into this world to be its light, so we (the post Jesus' death and resurrection people) are handed the torch and therein are covenanted with the same role, that of being light to the world.

Acts 13:47 states: "For so the Lord has commanded us: 'I have set you as a light to the gentiles, that you should be for salvation to the ends of the Earth.'" Does this statement not make you tingle with excitement when you realize that you, yes you, are the light of the world? With the same powerful Holy Spirit anointing that made Jesus the light of the world, so you and I now possess the same title and role, that of, categorically, we are the light of the world. No wonder Jesus said that it was for our benefit that He departs in an expedited manner. Why? So that He could quickly pass the torch on to us. Now, instead of one source of light illuminating a world left to play host to the great controversy between good and evil, there could be thousands, if not millions of lights covering the globe.

The text also informs us of both what we will become as well as how far this role of being the light would take us. It states, "that you should be for salvation to the ends of the Earth." It is hard to imagine that our lives will literally be used "for the very salvation" of the world. This beautiful promise of a role worthy of an heir to God Himself, dovetails so wonderfully into the very gospel commission itself, that of Matthew 28:19, which reads: "Go therefore and make disciples of all the nations."

Interestingly, when Matthew wrote his gospel, he didn't slowly break the news to us as did John, rather, he got right to the point by stating: "You are the light of the world. A city that is set on a hill cannot be hidden" (Matthew 5:14).

You are the light of the world. It can't be made much plainer than that.

CHAPTER 13

ME AND MY HOUSE

S O WE ARE THE LIGHT OF THE WORLD, WHAT A GREAT HONOR it is to live on this side of the cross, where we are privileged beyond anyone else in biblical history, including John the Baptist, who was considered "not the light." Jesus set the stage and commenced the work that would finally wrap things up for this world and then, once He established the cause, He appointed us to be His representatives as lights in the world—an incredible thought!

The Laodiceans Again

How does this work? From the foundation of this earth, Jesus had a magnificent plan in place for every single person. Within that plan, He had an ideal of what He wanted to do and accomplish through each person. For you and me, Jesus planned that we would be lights in this world. There was to be great action, not some passive, boring life to live and then check out to a funeral home. No, if you still possess a beating heart, then Heaven still has a big plan for you.

Look again at the Laodiceans of Revelation 3:14–17. In Revelation 3:20 we find that the call to a connected life with Jesus is made to all, not just some. It states, "I stand at the door and knock. If anyone hears My voice and opens the door, I will come in to him and dine with him, and he with Me." It clearly states if *any,* meaning the invitation to connect is open to all, not just some. It is true that according to Matthew 22:14 many are "called" but few are "chosen." But that would indicate that there is some sort of selectivity in whom God chooses to engage in His service but put into full context, the reference can and should be read this way: "Few are chosen because few fully submit their entire agenda to Jesus."

I hear people quote the promise of Romans 8:28 and then wonder why it doesn't seem to come to fruition. It is a simple promise: "We know that all things work together for good to those who love God, to those who are the called according to His purpose." The problem is those who quote it also don't expect much from it, and generally ignore the fact that there are two conditions through which the promise can become reality. "All things will work together for good to those" who, firstly, harbor a deep love for God and, secondly, "are the called according to his purpose."

The "called according to his purpose" part again has everything to do with step three, that of giving your life fully over to Jesus. To be called according to His purpose means to submit your agenda to the control of Jesus. So to think that "all things will work together for good," yet at the same not turning your life completely over to God to be used for His purpose, is to be living in a fantasy world of unrealistic as well as unbiblical expectations.

Total Submission

One doesn't have to look far to discover what God means when He says submit. In Luke 14:33 it states, "So likewise, whoever of you does not forsake all that he has cannot be My disciple." This verse is saying that there is to be no clinging to other perceived priorities if we are suggesting that we are giving up full control of our lives to Jesus. This text makes the point very clear: you will never become a disciple of Jesus as long as you choose to allow other distraction such as watching television, surfing the internet, playing video games or interacting with other people (including your own family) to take top priority.

Yes, even our own family. Matthew 10:37, 38 says: "He who loves father or mother more than Me is not worthy of Me. And he who loves son or daughter more than Me is not worthy of Me. And he who does not take his cross and follow after Me is not worthy of Me." Clearly, there is to be nothing of greater priority in your life than that of Jesus and Him crucified, if, that is, you desire to have the explosive relationship as promised.

God set the stage early through the Ten Commandments of Exodus 20 when His very first command says, "You shall have no other gods before Me" (Exodus 20:3). When properly interpreted, a god is anything or anybody that eclipses your commitment to Jesus. In the context of Matthew 10:37, 38, that can and does include your closest family. If your desire for a particular car, house or other material thing is at a passion-level higher than what you have for Jesus, then don't expect the relationship that sizzles. If you could be objective about your own self-analysis, would your love for your earthly father, mother, son, daughter, spouse, girlfriend or boyfriend etcetera, be of greater passion than that of what you have for God? If so, then according to the Bible, you are not totally submitted to Him.

Investment Portfolio

The Bible is boldly, if not bluntly, clear as to what level of submission and passionate pursuit God expects you to exercise if you are expecting to find and maintain a meaningful relationship with Jesus. Jesus Himself obviously desired us to understand this level of commitment when He told the parable of the "pearl of great price." We can read it in Matthew 13:45, 46 where He says, "Again, the kingdom of heaven is like a merchant seeking beautiful pearls, who, when he had found one pearl of great price, went and sold all that he had and bought it." In other words, give up absolutely everything you currently think is important and, in turn, exchange it in for a life one hundred percent committed to Jesus. Unfortunately very few people do this because it seems such a monumental sacrifice in exchange for what appears, on the surface anyway, a poor deal. If your perception of Christ-likeness is that you observe in the people of your church and the churches around you, then your assumption would be most likely entirely correct. The problem with drawing your point of view of God from that of what you see in those who proclaim to be Christians though, is according to the Bible, what you see is most definitely not what you get, if, that is, you have chosen to fully commit your life to Jesus' will.

The great news of it all, though, is to be found in Matthew 19:29. "And everyone who has left houses or brothers or sisters or father or mother or wife or children or lands, for My name's sake, shall receive a hundredfold, and inherit eternal life." What a promise! A massive return on investment is offered here. It states that we "shall receive a hundredfold" return on investment, to say nothing of the "eternal life" also offered.

My greatest interest in understanding this concept is more in line with the answer to the question, "When can I expect to see my return on investment?" Is it one of those things that comes along with the heaven and eternal life package, or is it something I can expect during this life?

First and foremost, heaven with its eternal life, against earth with its three score and ten average years of life, is not a measly one hundred times return on investment but rather the math function would be more appropriately represented as "infinity divided by 70 = infinity." So the one hundred percent return on time can't obviously refer to a reward that is to be issued much later, after the point where we go to heaven.

How about the quality of life we will live in heaven in comparison to the rat hole we live in now? Again, if heaven (according to 1 Corinthians 2:9), is to be of such incredible grandeur as to be out of the realm of anything we have ever seen or heard here on this earth, then its ratio would be trillions of times greater than what we could ever imagine to experience living here.

How about the potential for monetary gain in heaven being that of only one hundred times better than what we have here and now? One look at Revelation 21:21 and even the weakest of financial analyst's summaries would spell out the reality of it all—a heavenly return on investment, compared to what we have here on earth, is not on the same planet-of-comparison: "The twelve gates were twelve pearls: each individual gate was of one pearl. And the street of the city was pure gold, like transparent glass."

The point Jesus is attempting to get us to understand is this: If you choose to make Me your number one priority in life, I will give you a one hundred times return on your investment during this life "and" in addition to that, life eternal where a calculation of return on investment isn't remotely possible. The mere fact that the text uses the word "and" to separate the two different rewards ("shall receive an hundredfold, and shall inherit everlasting life") is indication that the one hundred times return on investment is to be claimed while on this earth and then, after that, we will be given an additional gift of "everlasting life."

Jesus is throwing out more than a subtle hint here. Rather, He is screaming through a megaphone: I want to bless you and reward you now. I want to give you an abundant life (John 10:10) in exchange for your undivided attention and submission.

Crucial Questions

You might ask, *How am I supposed to get to the level where my submission is so complete that I can be sure of these promises? Or, I would love to have what Jesus had with His Father and so completely turn my life over to Him that everything that happens in my life is clearly Him through me, but the ugly reality of it all is, I am not like Jesus, so how can anyone suggest that it is even possible for me in the first place?*

It is a good thing to ask questions because without the asking of questions there will be little need to seek answers. Questions inherently drive us, in the direction at least, to both our knees and to the Bible in search of answers. Then our minds will be open to be impacted by Jesus.

Romans 12:2 indicates just what needs to take place in our lives in order for submission to be even possible in the first place. It states "And do not be conformed to this world, but be transformed by the renewing of your mind, that you may prove what is that good and acceptable and perfect will of God." We need to focus on the last three words of this text. It references the very "will of God." We must recognize that every single thing Jesus did and/or said was the full manifestation of Him living under the umbrella of "not my will, but yours be done" (Luke 22:42).

If that is what Jesus did, then that is what we need to do. So we need to simply figure out how to get to the point where we can turn our complete agenda over to Jesus so that He can fully run our lives according to His will. Romans 12:2 quite clearly tells us how to get to the stage in life where we are living, full time, for Jesus, and not for ourselves. It says: "Be transformed by the renewing of your mind, that you may prove what is that good and acceptable and perfect will of God."

What is needed in order to acquire and maintain the dynamic, results-producing relationship with Jesus is a "renewing" of our minds from something old and moldy to something new and fresh. As we have seen, that will take place only by way of a serious amount of time spent in pursuit of and in the company of Jesus. Without knowing Jesus, there is no use praying for God's will to be done in your life because your life will not have the capacity to contain such supernatural power.

In Luke 5:37, 38 we are given a glimpse into the futility of attempting to tap into God's powers without first having rid ourselves of the old "us" and in turn becoming "transformed." It states: "And no one puts new wine into old wineskins; or else the new wine will burst the wineskins and be spilled, and the wineskins will be ruined. But new wine must be put into new wineskins, and both are preserved."

The point of this allegory should not be missed, as it is not so much about "new wine" as it is about "old bottles." Old bottles being, us, status quo Christians who become so inflexible through our centuries of going-through-the-motions traditions and preconceptions that there is no way the bubbling and efflorescence of a Savior of action, could do anything less than burst our little rigid bubbles with His very presence.

A rebirth, or new start, needs to take place in us whereby we become flexible and moldable so as to allow dynamic, divine movement to percolate inside us. The analogy of a potter shaping something soft and pliable into something of eternal value is precisely what the new life, in complete submission to Jesus, is all about. Romans 9:21 asks, "Does not the potter have power over the clay?" If it makes any sense at all that Jesus should have control over our lives, then we should pay heed to the statement of submission found in Isaiah 64:8—"But now, O Lord, You are our Father; We are the clay, and You our potter; and all we are the work of Your hand."

How can we be the work of Jesus' hand if we are old and dried up and nothing but rigid wine skins or rock-hard clumps of dirt? We need to first take in the "living water" as found in Jesus (John 4:10) so that it can impregnate us and turn us into malleable clay. We need to become new and flexible "wine skins" by starting all over with a rebirth. In John 3:3 Jesus laid out the prerequisite to becoming a flexible and malleable agent of Him by stating, "Most assuredly, I say to you, unless one is born again, he cannot see the kingdom of

God." You can't be reborn without the key to it all, that of ingesting mass quantities of the Word of God. 1 Peter 1:23 makes this point very clear where the apostle states: "having been born again, not of corruptible seed but incorruptible, *through the word of God* which lives and abides forever" (emphasis added).

Peter offers only one option in which to accomplish the seemingly unaccomplishable: drinking in of God's Holy Word. This living water will soak into all the dried and cracked recesses of our hardened souls and slowly but surely begin to saturate each clay particle. Then, as Satan begins his inevitable assault on us to deter us from such life-changing activity, his pushing, shoving and punching of us will, to his detriment, ultimately aid in blending the water with the clay particles and we will become soft and moldable and thus Jesus, the potter, can accept our commitment to submit to His will. He can then, in turn, take His nail-scarred hands and shape us into something of great beauty.

Declaration of Independence (from Self, Sin, and Satan)

I often have people ask me what a statement of commitment may sound like and more pointedly what do I do or say in my daily commitment to Jesus. I must admit that this is a rather intimate and personal subject that is generally kept as a private matter, but for the purpose of offering a mere suggestion, I will share what I typically audibly (meaning out loud) declare. It goes something like this:

Father God in Heaven, as I stand here this morning, before you, the Creator of the Universe, I wish to declare, and make public, a statement of my allegiance to the King of kings and Lord of lords, the God and creator of the Universe. I declare through the power found in the blood, shed on my behalf by my dear Savior, Jesus, that Satan be muted from uttering any accusation of unfairness through what I claim as a blood brother to Jesus. I hereby declare in whom I will serve and submit to. I declare in no uncertain terms, as Joshua did thousands of years ago, that as for me and my house, we will serve the Lord God Almighty.

It is to be understood by the universe that God is my one and only Master. Through the blood of Jesus, I declare that as my Master, I give Him full right to take absolute control of my life. By way of control I mean I give my thoughts to Him; I give to Him all the decisions I will need to make today; I give my motivations to Him today. I declare that I wish for my Master to take away all elements of my pride and in turn replace it with humility. I leave myself fully open to Him as a piece of malleable clay to be worked as He needs and desires so that my life can be an extension of Him in delivering His compassion to a lost world. I ask for the right to be given the eyes of Jesus so that I can look deeply into the souls of all those whom I come in contact with today and to be given divine discernment to know and perceive what words of comfort that they will need, in order to fill the void that limits their lives. I ask in the name of Jesus that I will be given boldness beyond my human tendency so that I may lift up Jesus to the lost so that they may be drawn to Him by Him.

As is my right, I ask that I be given the full presence and power of the Holy Spirit so that wherever I go today and whomever I meet, that His presence will precede me so that hearts will be prepared for the good news You wish to share through me. I declare this morning that what I am claiming is fully fair in the great controversy between God and Satan because I make this statement of claim and intent both in the name of Jesus as well as the power in the blood He shed for me and those I come in contact with today.

Consequently, there are to be no accusations filed by Satan or his evil angels towards either God or myself, as this statement of allegiance is fully my free choice to make. May it now be known before the universe that I proceed with my day under the power of the master I choose to have control my life, that of God, the Father, Jesus, His Son and the Holy Spirit.

Since the third step in having and maintaining a dynamic relationship with Jesus is that of submitting our wills to Jesus, we can expect something incredible to happen during our day under such commitment. The mere fact that I audibly make such a statement makes me much more keenly aware of my surroundings, particularly the people I will come in contact with that day. I have discovered that when I pray, from the depths of my heart, the above-type public prayer, a change takes place in my heart. I look to my day with a sense of adventure and expectation, not knowing what or how God will choose to use me.

The mere thought that even my day is now anointed, in and of itself, gives me a sense of great destiny which, in turn, directly influences my level of confidence which again, in turn, gives me an attitude of, *I am in possession of greater power than have most people in society.* These mental attributes alone greatly benefit me in business and in the interpersonal relationships I have with my clients.

Interactions

When I share with my clients what I am all about, that my life has changed radically for the good after taking God on as a business partner, when I share that if God wants me to have this project with you, my customer, then I will have it, or if not, then I don't want it anyhow. When I add to that statement that if God does want me to have the job, then I can guarantee that there will not be another engineering firm on the planet that will be able to design a solution even close to the solution we will be able to deliver to you—they are left with one of two options: (1) this guy is "nuts," or (2) he truly does have something above and beyond the rest who are pursuing the job. My sales pitch is no longer an "apples against apples" comparison with my competitors. Rather, I am immediately put into a different category—one that forces the client to weigh the potential source of my boldness and great confidence combined with an attitude of, *I don't really care what decision you come to, as I believe it is in God's hands anyhow.*

No question, much is to be gained in turning one's life over to the control of Someone bigger—Someone you've learned to trust with your life. By doing so, you remove responsibility for taking care of yourself, since it becomes Someone else's burden, not your own. You are thereby able to bask in the most elusive state of being—that of being fully content with life. If your life is out of your hands, then there's nothing to worry about, because you no longer have to be responsible for something that Someone else bigger than yourself has promised to protect and take care of. And then when you begin observing your own life impacting the lives of others in a positive way, and you realize that it is beyond your human skill-set or natural character that these good things are taking place, you will quickly come to the humbling realization that God in Heaven is real.

In Conclusion . . .

The real bottom line is that, if anyone can walk away from having engaged themselves in an intense reading of the Book of Acts and not leave disillusioned at the huge chasm that exists between the then and the now, then quite frankly they have probably succumbed to the deadly conclusion that the epitome of what God has planned for us today, is exactly what we observe taking place in the churches we attend. If the churches we attend are dead and lifeless, if they have limited impact on their associated surrounding communities, if its individual members have become separatists by way of pretty much associating only with fellow attendees and not reaching out to a lost and hurting community—then is the church, or for that matter, its members, really the beacons of light, as portrayed in Matthew 5:14–16?

When it says, "You [the church or individually] are the light of the world. A city that is set on a hill cannot be hid," does it not connote something that is to be a dominant, observable force in the community? If instead, the lights in a church are only those of the electrically powered, incandescent type, and they are observable only during a couple of services a week—church and/or prayer meeting times—then the point has been completely missed.

A lighthouse is of no value to a ship on a tempestuous sea if only its internal lights are switched on so that its occupants can carry on with their own little micro-lives. No, a lighthouse is meant to emit a bright, fog-piercing beam of penetrating light to allow a floundering and lost humanity to find its direction in the darkness as found in the world. Individual members are to be seen as fully energized points-of-direction so that others can navigate their lives based on those whose true, representative name tag says, *Christian.*

In short, I have discovered, in only a small way, that there is a whole other realm of living, a realm that links us, the human, with the divine. The process is called "rebirth." It is a rebirth into the form of a baby whose total dependence and submission is to those who, through love, conceived and gave birth to him or her. Our parent in Heaven—God, Jesus, and the Holy Spirit—eagerly awaits this spiritual rebirth in each of us, so that He can legitimately pour out His desire to bless us, just as one's own parents would give good things to their own children. So hungry and anxious is God for this kind of a family connection with us His creation that He gave up His own Son in exchange for our adoption.

In Matthew 7:9–11 Jesus goes to great lengths to inform us of what His Father has in store for us: "What man is there among you who, if his son asks for bread, will give him a stone? Or if he asks for a fish, will he give him a serpent? If you then, being evil, know how to give good gifts to your children, how much more will your Father who is in heaven give good things to those who ask Him!"

Right now, upon completion of reading this how-to book, one would hope that the following questions of eternal destiny would be encroaching upon a mind used to putting off decisions. These questions beg to be answered in a manner of action, not simply a verbal "yes" or cerebral assent.

Is the eternal Heavenly reward worth the temporal earthly effort?

Is an hour a day with Jesus, our Savior, too much of an imposition to our normally busy lives, an absolute critical element to connecting, in a relationship, with Jesus? Is my Lord and Savior, Jesus, worth the effort?

And if so, why not follow the lead of Joshua and boldly declare before your family and friends, to the whole world: "Me and my house, we will serve the Lord!"

MY CHALLENGE

IT MUST BE STATED THAT THERE EXISTS NO GREATER ENDORSE-ment for anything we may try or experience in life than that of the personal testimony of what took place in our own lives. The Bible is clear that there is power in the sharing of one's personal testimony, in fact, so much power that it is one of two weapons identified in Revelation 12:11—"They overcame him by the blood of the Lamb, and by the word of *their testimony*; and they loved not their lives unto the death" (emphasis added)—that are used by the victorious saints in Heaven to defeat Satan and his evil forces.

While the words of the age-old Bible are unquestionably power-ful, there exists an extra lethal bullet to Satan's agenda when the followers of Jesus elevate their Savior (John 12:32) through boldly sharing what He has done for them. It is the personal story of the "cause and effect" of submitting to a God who delights in giving good things to His children that most effectively proves the reality of His existence to a lost and broken world.

To this point, I wish to add the fact that I receive hundreds of emails and letters from people around the world who have graciously taken the time to share their personal stories of their lives changed through taking the challenge of spending an hour a day with Jesus. Interestingly, these written personal testimonies virtually all commence with the words: "You will not believe what is happening in my life . . ." and then go on to enthusiastically explain the amazing transformations that have enveloped their lives.

It is through these many stories that real proof is delivered , and that without question proves that the only means of securing and maintaining a relationship with Jesus is though a serious amount of time spent pursuing Him. This clear evidence cannot be overlooked or taken for granted, as it quite frankly and boldly states that "there are no shortcuts available in which to develop a dynamic, results-producing relationship with the Savior who died for you and me."

As a resultant the question that you, the reader of this book now needs to ask yourself is simply this: *Is Jesus worth the effort?*

The challenge delivered through the personal testimonies of the thousands whose lives have changed through spending an hour a day with Jesus should provide more than enough proof that, yes, He is most definitely worth the effort.

So, "Grace be with you all. Amen" (Hebrews 13:25).

* * * * *

HERB LARSEN MINISTRIES

Herb Larsen Jr. maintains a world-wide speaking schedule across a range of faiths, venues and audiences. He presents in variety of situations including churches, schools and colleges, business and church conferences and seminars.

For more information or to inquire:

UNITED STATES OF AMERICA
PO Box 357
Sumas, Washington 98 295
U.S.A.

CANADA
35276 Rockwell Dr
Abbotsford, British Columbia V3G 2C9
Canada

AUSTRALIA
PO Box 306
Thornleigh, NSW 2120
Australia

EMAIL
herblarsenministries.org

WEB
herblarsenministries.com